interchange
FOURTH EDITION

Jack C. Richards

With Jonathan Hull and Susan Proctor

Series Editor: David Bohlke

CAMBRIDGE
UNIVERSITY PRESS

STUDENT'S BOOK **2A**

CAMBRIDGE UNIVERSITY PRESS
Cambridge, New York, Melbourne, Madrid, Cape Town,
Singapore, São Paulo, Delhi, Mexico City

Cambridge University Press
32 Avenue of the Americas, New York, NY 10013-2473, USA

www.cambridge.org
Information on this title: www.cambridge.org/9781107637191

First published 2006
3rd printing 2013

Printed in Lima, Peru, by Empresa Editora El Comercio S.A.

A catalog record for this publication is available from the British Library.

ISBN 978-1-107-64869-2 Student's Book 2 with Self-study DVD-ROM
ISBN 978-1-107-64410-6 Student's Book 2A with Self-study DVD-ROM
ISBN 978-1-107-62676-8 Student's Book 2B with Self-study DVD-ROM
ISBN 978-1-107-64873-9 Workbook 2
ISBN 978-1-107-61698-1 Workbook 2A
ISBN 978-1-107-65075-6 Workbook 2B
ISBN 978-1-107-62527-3 Teacher's Edition 2 with Assessment Audio CD/CD-ROM
ISBN 978-1-107-62941-7 Class Audio 2 CDs
ISBN 978-1-107-62500-6 Full Contact 2 with Self-study DVD-ROM
ISBN 978-1-107-63719-1 Full Contact 2A with Self-study DVD-ROM
ISBN 978-1-107-65092-3 Full Contact 2B with Self-study DVD-ROM

For a full list of components, visit www.cambridge.org/interchange

Art direction, book design, layout services, and photo research: Integra
Audio production: CityVox, NYC
Video production: Nesson Media Boston, Inc.

Welcome to *Interchange Fourth Edition*, the world's most successful English series!

Interchange offers a complete set of tools for learning how to communicate in English.

Student's Book
with **NEW Self-study DVD-ROM**

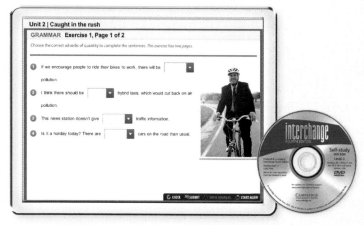

- **Complete video program** with additional **video exercises**

- Additional **vocabulary**, **grammar**, **speaking**, **listening**, and **reading** practice
- Printable **score reports** to submit to teachers

Available online

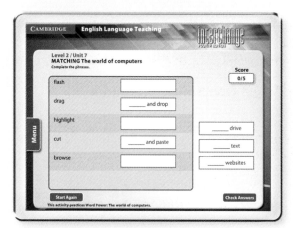

Interchange Arcade

- **Free** self-study website
- **Fun**, interactive, self-scoring activities
- Practice **vocabulary**, **grammar**, **listening**, and **reading**
- **MP3s** of the class audio program

Online Workbook

- A variety of **interactive activities** that correspond to each Student's Book lesson
- **Instant feedback** for hundreds of activities
- **Easy to use** with clear, easy-to-follow instructions
- Extra **listening practice**
- Simple tools for teachers to **monitor progress** such as scores, attendance, and time spent online

Authors' acknowledgments

A great number of people contributed to the development of *Interchange Fourth Edition*. Particular thanks are owed to the reviewers using *Interchange, Third Edition* in the following schools and institutes – their insights and suggestions have helped define the content and format of the fourth edition:

Ian Geoffrey Hanley, **The Address Education Center**, Izmir, Turkey

James McBride, **AUA Language Center**, Bangkok, Thailand

Jane Merivale, **Centennial College**, Toronto, Ontario, Canada

Elva Elena Peña Andrade, **Centro de Auto Aprendizaje de Idiomas**, Nuevo León, Mexico

José Paredes, **Centro de Educación Continua de la Escuela Politécnica Nacional** (CEC-EPN), Quito, Ecuador

Chia-jung Tsai, **Changhua University of Education**, Changhua City, Taiwan

Kevin Liang, **Chinese Culture University**, Taipei, Taiwan

Roger Alberto Neira Perez, **Colegio Santo Tomás de Aquino**, Bogotá, Colombia

Teachers at **Escuela Miguel F. Martínez**, Monterrey, Mexico

Maria Virgínia Goulart Borges de Lebron, **Great Idiomas**, São Paulo, Brazil

Gina Kim, **Hoseo University**, Chungnam, South Korea

Heeyong Kim, Seoul, South Korea

Elisa Borges, **IBEU-Rio**, Rio de Janeiro, Brazil

Jason M. Ham, **Inha University**, Incheon, South Korea

Rita de Cássia S. Silva Miranda, **Instituto Batista de Idiomas**, Belo Horizonte, Brazil

Teachers at **Instituto Politécnico Nacional**, Mexico City, Mexico

Victoria M. Roberts and Regina Marie Williams, **Interactive College of Technology**, Chamblee, Georgia, USA

Teachers at **Internacional de Idiomas**, Mexico City, Mexico

Marcelo Serafim Godinho, **Life Idiomas**, São Paulo, Brazil

J. Kevin Varden, **Meiji Gakuin University**, Yokohama, Japan

Rosa Maria Valencia Rodríguez, Mexico City, Mexico

Chung-Ju Fan, **National Kinmen Institute of Technology**, Kinmen, Taiwan

Shawn Beasom, **Nihon Daigaku**, Tokyo, Japan

Gregory Hadley, **Niigata University of International and Information Studies**, Niigata, Japan

Chris Ruddenklau, **Osaka University of Economics and Law**, Osaka, Japan

Byron Roberts, **Our Lady of Providence Girls' High School**, Xindian City, Taiwan

Simon Banha, **Phil Young's English School**, Curitiba, Brazil

Flávia Gonçalves Carneiro Braathen, **Real English Center**, Viçosa, Brazil

Márcia Cristina Barboza de Miranda, **SENAC**, Recife, Brazil

Raymond Stone, **Seneca College of Applied Arts and Technology**, Toronto, Ontario, Canada

Gen Murai, **Takushoku University**, Tokyo, Japan

Teachers at **Tecnológico de Estudios Superiores de Ecatepec**, Mexico City, Mexico

Teachers at **Universidad Autónoma Metropolitana– Azcapotzalco**, Mexico City, Mexico

Teachers at **Universidad Autónoma de Nuevo León**, Monterrey, Mexico

Mary Grace Killian Reyes, **Universidad Autónoma de Tamaulipas**, Tampico Tamaulipas, Mexico

Teachers at **Universidad Estatal del Valle de Ecatepec**, Mexico City, Mexico

Teachers at **Universidad Nacional Autónoma de Mexico – Zaragoza**, Mexico City, Mexico

Teachers at **Universidad Nacional Autónoma de Mexico – Iztacala**, Mexico City, Mexico

Luz Edith Herrera Diaz, Veracruz, Mexico

Seri Park, **YBM PLS**, Seoul, South Korea

Self-assessment charts revised by Alex Tilbury

Grammar plus written by Karen Davy

Plan of Book 2A

A time to remember

1 **SNAPSHOT**

Friend Finder

Search

Ted Johnson

Sex: Male
Current city: Los Angeles, California, U.S.A.
Hometown: Dallas, Texas, U.S.A

Contact information
Email: ted.johnson@cup.org

Education and Work
College: Farrington Technical Institute, Dallas
Employer: Deluxe Tours

Likes and interests
I love to be outdoors. I enjoy skiing and swimming. And I'm a good cook.

Ana Fernandez

Sex: Female
Current city: Los Angeles, California, U.S.A.
Hometown: Buenos Aires, Argentina

Contact information
Email: a_fernandez@email.com

Education and Work
High school: Santa Maria High School, Los Angeles
Employer: Sports Unlimited

Likes and interests
I like to go to the movies and take long walks. And I'm learning to in-line skate!

Do you think Ted and Ana could be friends?
Is social networking popular in your country? Do you use any sites? Which ones?
Create your own online profile and compare it with a partner. How are you the same? different?

2 **CONVERSATION** *Where did you learn to skate?*

A ▶ Listen and practice.

Ted: Oh, I'm really sorry. Are you OK?
Ana: I'm fine. But I'm not very good at this.
Ted: Neither am I. . . . Hey, I like your shirt. Are you from Argentina?
Ana: Yes, I am, originally. I was born there.
Ted: Did you grow up there?
Ana: Yes, I did, but my family moved here ten years ago, when I was in middle school.
Ted: And where did you learn to skate?
Ana: Here in the park. This is only my third time.
Ted: Well, it's my *first* time. Can you give me some lessons?
Ana: Sure. Just follow me.
Ted: By the way, my name is Ted.
Ana: And I'm Ana. Nice to meet you.

B ▶ Listen to the rest of the conversation. What are two more things you learn about Ted?

GRAMMAR FOCUS

> **Past tense** ⊙
>
> Where **were** you born? When **did** you **move** to Los Angeles?
>   I **was** born in Argentina.   I **moved** here ten years ago. I **didn't speak** English.
> **Were** you born in Buenos Aires? **Did** you **take** English classes in Argentina?
>   Yes, I **was**.   Yes, I **did**. I **took** classes for a year.
>   No, I **wasn't**. I **was** born in Córdoba.   No, I **didn't**. My aunt **taught** me at home.

A Complete these conversations. Then practice with a partner.

1. A: Could you tell me a little about yourself?
    Where .... you born?
    B: I .... born in South Korea.
    A: .... you grow up there?
    B: No, I .... I .... up in Canada.

2. A: When .... you begin to study English?
    B: I .... in middle school.
    A: What .... you think of English class
    at first?
    B: I .... it was a little difficult, but fun.

3. A: .... you have a favorite teacher when
    you .... a child?
    B: Yes, I .... I .... an excellent
    teacher named Miss Perez.
    A: What .... she teach?
    B: She .... science.

B **PAIR WORK** Take turns asking the questions in
part A. Give your own information when answering.

LISTENING *Life as an immigrant*

A ⊙ Listen to interviews with two immigrants to the
United States. Where are they from?

B ⊙ Listen again and complete the chart.

	Huy	Ahmed
1. When did he move to the United States?		
2. What is difficult about being an immigrant?		
3. What does he miss the most?		

5 SPEAKING Tell me about yourself.

A PAIR WORK Check (✓) six questions below. Then interview a classmate you don't know very well. Ask follow-up questions.

- ☐ Where did you go to middle school?
- ☐ Were you a good student in middle school?
- ☐ What were your best subjects?
- ☐ What subjects didn't you like?
- ☐ When did you first study English?

- ☐ What other languages can you speak?
- ☐ Do you have a big family?
- ☐ Did you enjoy your childhood?
- ☐ Did you have a pet?
- ☐ Who was your hero when you were a child?

A: What were your best subjects in middle school?
B: My best subjects were science and math.
A: Really? Me, too! Did you get good grades in English?

B GROUP WORK Tell the group what you learned about your partner. Then answer any questions.

"In middle school, Ji-won got good grades in science and math, but he didn't do very well in . . . "

useful expressions
Oh, that's interesting. Really? Me, too! Wow! Tell me more.

6 WORD POWER

A Complete the word map. Add two more words of your own to each category. Then compare with a partner.

✓ beach
cat
collect comic books
crayons
fish
play soccer
play video games
playground
rabbit
scrapbook
summer camp
toys

Pets

Hobbies

Childhood memories

Places
beach

Possessions

B PAIR WORK Choose three words from the word map and use them to describe some of your childhood memories.

A: I had a scrapbook when I was little.
B: What did you keep in it?
A: I kept lots of things in it. It had some school awards, photos, and notes from my friends.

7 PERSPECTIVES *How have you changed?*

A ▶ Listen to these statements about changes. Check (✓) those that are true about you.

☐ **1.** "When I was a kid, I used to be very messy, but now I'm very neat."

☐ **2.** "I didn't use to collect anything, but now I do."

☐ **3.** "I never used to play sports, but now I like to keep fit."

☐ **4.** "I never used to worry about money, but I do now."

☐ **5.** "I used to have a lot of hobbies, but now I don't have any free time."

☐ **6.** "I didn't use to follow politics, but now I check headlines online every day."

☐ **7.** "When I was younger, I used to care a lot about my appearance. Now, I'm too busy to care how I look."

B **PAIR WORK** Look at the statements again. Which changes are positive? Which are negative?

"I think the first one is a positive change. It's good to be neat."

8 GRAMMAR FOCUS

> ### Used to ▶
>
> **Used to** *refers to something that you regularly did in the past but don't do anymore.*
>
> **Did** you **use to** collect things?
>   Yes, I **used to** collect comic books.
>   No, I **didn't use to** collect anything,
>   but now I collect art.
>
> What sports **did** you **use to** play?
>   I **used to play** baseball and volleyball.
>   I **never used to** play sports, but now I
>   play tennis.

A Complete these questions and answers. Then compare with a partner.

1. A: ....Did.... you ....use to........ collect comic books when you were little?
   B: No, I .... collect comic books.

2. A: .... you and your friends .... play at the playground as kids?
   B: Yes, we .... spend hours there on the weekends.

3. A: What video games .... you .... play?
   B: I .... play video games. But now I play them all the time!

4. A: What music .... you .... listen to?
   B: I .... listen to pop music a lot, but now I prefer rock.

B How have you changed? Write six sentences about yourself using *used to* or *didn't use to*.

your hairstyle   your taste in music
your hobbies   the way you dress

> I used to wear my hair much longer.
> I didn't use to wear it short.

9 PRONUNCIATION Used to

A ▶ Listen and practice. Notice that the pronunciation of **used to** and **use to** is the same.

When I was a child, I **used to** play the trumpet.
I **used to** have a nickname.
I didn't **use to** like scary movies.
I didn't **use to** study very hard at school.

B **PAIR WORK** Practice the sentences you wrote in Exercise 8, part B. Pay attention to the pronunciation of **used to** and **use to**.

10 SPEAKING Memories

A **PAIR WORK** Add three questions to this list. Then take turns asking and answering the questions.

1. What's your favorite childhood memory?
2. What sports or games did you use to play when you were younger?
3. Did you use to have a nickname?
4. Where did you use to spend your vacations?
5. Is your taste in music different now?
6. ....
7. ....
8. ....

B **CLASS ACTIVITY** Tell the class two interesting things about your partner.

11 WRITING About myself

A Write a paragraph about things you used to do as a child. Use some of your ideas from Exercise 10. Just for fun, include one false statement.

> When I was four years old, my family moved to Australia. We had an old two-story house and a big yard. My older brother and I used to play lots of games together. In the summer, my favorite outdoor game was . . .

B **GROUP WORK** Share your paragraphs and answer any questions. Can you find the false statements?

12 INTERCHANGE 1 Class profile

Find out more about your classmates. Go to Interchange 1 on page 114.

DREW BARRYMORE — Actor, Producer, Director

Scan the article. Where was Drew Barrymore born? When did she start working? When did she win the Golden Globe Award?

Drew Barrymore was born in Los Angeles, California, in 1975. She comes from a long line of actors. In fact, her grandfather, John Barrymore, was one of the most famous actors in the United States in the 1920s.

Drew Barrymore began her career very early. Before her first birthday, she appeared in a TV commercial for dog food. At the age of two, she acted in her first TV movie. At age five, she appeared in her first feature film, the sci-fi thriller *Altered States*.

Barrymore's big break came two years later, at age seven. Director Steven Spielberg decided to cast her in his film *E.T.: The Extra-Terrestrial*. Hollywood took notice, and Drew became a star.

As a young adult, Barrymore acted in several dramas and romantic comedies; however, she wanted to make her own films. In 1995, she started her own production company, Flower Films. Four years later, she produced her first film, *Never Been Kissed*. Over the years, her company has made a lot of famous movies and TV programs, including *Fever Pitch* in 2005 and the new *Charlie's Angels* TV series in 2011.

In 2007, Barrymore's career took a new turn. She began working for the United Nations World Food Programme. Later, she donated $1 million to the program. Then, after a terrible earthquake in Haiti in 2010, she urged people to give money to the program in a YouTube video.

Meanwhile, Barrymore's work on movies continued. In 2009, she became a director with the film *Whip It*. In the same year, she won the Golden Globe Award as an actress for her role in *Grey Gardens*.

Drew Barrymore wears many different hats and works very long hours. What does she do in her free time? She spends time with the people she cares about. She says, "I don't know what I'd do without my friends."

A Read the article. Find the words in *italics* below in the article. Then circle the meaning of each word or phrase.

1. When you get a *big break*, you experience a sudden **advance / accident**.
2. To *cast* an actor means to **hire / fire** the actor.
3. A *production company* **trains young actors / makes films.**
4. If you *urged* someone to do something, you **encouraged / discouraged** him or her.
5. When an actor plays a *role* in a film, he or she **wins an award / acts as another person.**
6. When someone *wears many different hats*, he or she **does a lot of different jobs / wins a lot of different awards.**

B Number these sentences about Drew Barrymore from 1 (first event) to 10 (last event).

.... a. She became a film director.
.... b. She became a film producer.
.... c. She gave away $1 million.
.... d. She was in a TV commercial.
....1.... e. She was born in California.
.... f. She started working for the United Nations.
.... g. She got her first role in a feature film.
.... h. She produced the movie *Fever Pitch*.
.... i. She became very famous as a child actor.
.... j. She started her own production company.

C PAIR WORK Who is your favorite actor or actress? What do you know about his or her life and career?

2 Caught in the rush

1 WORD POWER Compound nouns

A Match the words in columns A and B to make compound nouns. (More than one combination may be possible.)

subway + station = subway station

A	B
bicycle	garage
bus	jam
news	lane
parking	light
street	space
subway	stand
taxi	station
traffic	stop
train	system

a taxi stand

a bicycle lane

B PAIR WORK Which of these things can you find where you live?

A: There is a bus system here.
B: Yes. There are also a lot of traffic jams.

2 PERSPECTIVES Transportation services

A ▶ Listen to these comments about transportation services. Match them to the correct pictures.

_____ 1. "The buses are old and slow, and they cause too much pollution. In cities with less pollution, people are healthier."

_____ 2. "There are too many cars. All the cars, taxis, and buses are a danger to bicyclists. There is too much traffic!"

_____ 3. "There should be fewer cars, but I think that the biggest problem is parking. There just isn't enough parking."

B PAIR WORK Does your city or town have problems with traffic, pollution, and parking? What do you think is the biggest problem?

GRAMMAR FOCUS

Expressions of quantity ▶

With count nouns	**With noncount nouns**
There are **too many** cars.	There is **too much** traffic.
There should be **fewer** cars.	There should be **less** pollution.
We need **more** subway lines.	We need **more** public transportation.
There are**n't enough** buses.	There is**n't enough** parking.

A Complete these statements about transportation problems. Then compare with a partner. (More than one answer may be possible.)

1. There are .... police officers.
2. There should be .... cars in the city.
3. There is .... public transportation.
4. The government needs to build .... highways.
5. There should be .... noise.
6. The city needs .... public parking garages.
7. There is .... air pollution in the city.
8. There are .... cars parked on the streets.

B PAIR WORK Write sentences about the city or town you are living in. Then compare with another pair.

1. The city should provide more . . .
2. We have too many . . .
3. There's too much . . .
4. There isn't enough . . .
5. There should be fewer . . .
6. We don't have enough . . .
7. There should be less . . .
8. We need more . . .

LISTENING *Singapore solves it.*

A ▶ Listen to a resident of Singapore talk about how his city has tried to solve its traffic problems. Check (✓) True or False for each statement.

True	False		
☐	✓	**1.** Motorists can't drive into the business district.	*They need a pass to drive there.*
☐	☐	**2.** People need a special certificate to buy a car.	....
☐	☐	**3.** There are enough certificates for everyone.	....
☐	☐	**4.** Cars are more expensive than in North America.	....
☐	☐	**5.** Public transportation isn't very good.	....

B ▶ Listen again. For the false statements, write the correct information.

C CLASS ACTIVITY Could the solutions adopted in Singapore work in your city or town? Why or why not?

5 DISCUSSION *You be the judge!*

A GROUP WORK Which of these transportation services are available in your city or town? Discuss what is good and bad about each one.

.... taxi service   .... the subway system   .... facilities for pedestrians
.... the bus system   .... the train system   .... parking

B GROUP WORK How would you rate the transportation services where you live? Give each item a rating from 1 to 5.

1 = terrible   2 = needs improvement   3 = average   4 = good   5 = excellent

A: I'd give the taxi service a 4. There are enough taxis, but there
   are too many bad drivers.
B: I think a rating of 4 is too high. There should be more taxi stands and . . .

6 WRITING *An online post*

A Read this post from a community message board about traffic in the city.

B Use your statements from Exercise 3, part B, and any new ideas to write a message about a local issue.

C GROUP WORK Take turns reading your messages. Do you have any of the same concerns?

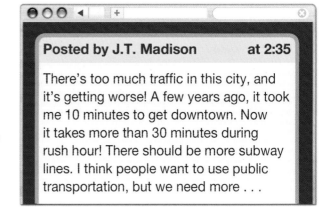

Posted by J.T. Madison   **at 2:35**

There's too much traffic in this city, and it's getting worse! A few years ago, it took me 10 minutes to get downtown. Now it takes more than 30 minutes during rush hour! There should be more subway lines. I think people want to use public transportation, but we need more . . .

7 SNAPSHOT

Common Questions
Asked by Visitors to a City

☐ How much do taxis cost?
☐ Where should I go shopping?
☐ Where can I get a map?
☐ What's the best way to see the city?
☐ Where can I buy a prepaid phone?

☐ Where's a good place to meet friends?
☐ What festivals or events are taking place?
☐ What are some family-friendly activities?
☐ Which hotel is closest to the airport?
☐ What museums should I see?

Sources: www.choosechicago.com; www.timessquarenyc.org

Check (✓) the questions you can answer about your city.
What other questions could a visitor ask about your city?
Talk to your classmates. Find answers to the questions you didn't check.

8 CONVERSATION *Could you tell me...?*

A ▶ Listen and practice.

Eric: Excuse me. Could you tell me where the nearest ATM is?

Clerk: There's one upstairs, across from the duty-free shop.

Eric: Great. And do you know where I can catch a bus to the city?

Clerk: Sure. Just follow the signs for "Transportation."

Eric: OK. And can you tell me how often they run?

Clerk: They run every 20 minutes or so.

Eric: And just one more thing. Do you know where the restrooms are?

Clerk: Right behind you. Do you see where that sign is?

Eric: Oh. Thanks a lot.

B ▶ Listen to the rest of the conversation.
Check (✓) the information that Eric asks for.

☐ the cost of a bus to the city   ☐ the cost of a guidebook
☐ the location of a taxi stand   ☐ the location of a bookstore

9 GRAMMAR FOCUS

> ### Indirect questions from Wh-questions ▶
>
> | **Wh-questions with be** | **Indirect questions** |
> | --- | --- |
> | Where is the nearest ATM? | Could you tell me **where the nearest ATM is**? |
> | Where are the restrooms? | Do you know **where the restrooms are**? |
>
> | **Wh-questions with do** | **Indirect questions** |
> | --- | --- |
> | How often do the buses run? | Can you tell me **how often the buses run**? |
> | What time does the bookstore open? | Do you know **what time the bookstore opens**? |
>
> | **Wh-questions with can** | **Indirect questions** |
> | --- | --- |
> | Where can I catch the bus? | Do you know **where I can catch the bus**? |

A Write indirect questions using these Wh-questions. Then compare with a partner.

1. How much does the bus cost?
2. Where's the nearest Internet café?
3. What time do the banks open?
4. How late do the buses run?
5. Where can I get a quick meal?
6. How late do the nightclubs stay open?
7. How early do the trains run?
8. Where's an inexpensive hotel in this area?

B **PAIR WORK** Take turns asking the questions you wrote in part A. Give your own information when answering.

"Can you tell me how much the bus costs?"

10 PRONUNCIATION *Syllable stress*

A ▶ Listen and practice. Notice which syllable has the main stress in these two-syllable words.

◗ ○   ○ ◗

subway   garage
traffic   police

B ▶ Listen to the stress in these words. Write them in the correct columns. Then compare with a partner.

◗ ○   ○ ◗

buses   improve   ....
bookstore provide   ....
event   public   ....
hotel   taxis   ....

11 SPEAKING *What do you know?*

A Complete the chart with indirect questions.

	Name: ....
1. Where's the nearest bus stop? " *Do you know where* .... ?"	
2. What's the best way to see the city? " .... ?"	
3. Where can I rent a bicycle? " .... ?"	
4. How much does a city tour cost? " .... ?"	
5. Where can I get a student discount on a meal? " .... ?"	
6. What time do the museums open? " .... ?"	
7. Where can I hear live music? " .... ?"	

B PAIR WORK Use the indirect questions in the chart to interview a classmate about the city or town where you live. Take notes.

A: Do you know where the nearest bus stop is?
B: I'm not really sure, but I think there's one . . .

C CLASS ACTIVITY Share your answers with the class. Who knows the most about your city or town?

12 INTERCHANGE 2 *Tourism campaign*

Discuss ways to attract tourists to a city. Go to Interchange 2 on page 115.

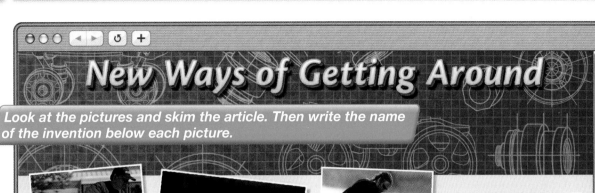

New Ways of Getting Around

Look at the pictures and skim the article. Then write the name of the invention below each picture.

Here are some of the best new inventions for getting around.

If you love to take risks when you travel, this is for you: the **Wheelman**. The design is simple: two wheels and a motor. You put your feet in the wheels. It's very similar to skateboarding or surfing. You use your weight to steer, and you control the speed with a ball you hold in your hand.

Why use two wheels when you can use three? The **Trikke Scooter** looks a little silly, but it's serious transportation. The three wheels make it very stable. And because it's made of aluminum, it's very light. It moves by turning back and forth – just like skiing on the street.

Do you want an eco-friendly family car? If so, check out the **Leaf**. It's all-electric and gives off zero CO_2 emissions. It has an 80 kW motor and can travel up to 140 kph! You can recharge the battery up to 80 percent of capacity in just 30 minutes and recharge it fully overnight.

To get around town in style and park easily, there's nothing better than the **Twizy Z.E.** It has four wheels, but it's only 2.3 meters long and 1.13 meters wide – the passenger sits behind the driver. It has a zero-emission 15 kW electric motor that can reach a maximum speed of 75 kph.

A Read the article. Where do you think it is from? Check (✓) the correct answer.

☐ an instruction manual ☐ a catalog ☐ a news magazine ☐ an encyclopedia

B Answer these questions.

1. Which inventions have motors? ....
2. Where do you put your feet in the Wheelman? ....
3. How do you steer the Wheelman? ....
4. What is the Trikke Scooter made of? ....
5. How does the Trikke Scooter move? ....
6. How long does it take to fully recharge the Leaf? ....
7. How long is the Twizy Z.E.? ....
8. Where does the passenger sit in the Twizy Z.E.? ....

C **GROUP WORK** Which of the inventions is the most useful? the least useful? Why? Would you like to try any of them?

Units 1–2 Progress check

SELF-ASSESSMENT

How well can you do these things? Check (✓) the boxes.

I can	Very well	OK	A little
Understand descriptions of childhood (Ex. 1)	☐	☐	☐
Ask and answer questions about childhood and past times (Ex. 1, 2)	☐	☐	☐
Express opinions about cities and towns; agree and disagree (Ex. 3)	☐	☐	☐
Ask for and give information about a city or town (Ex. 4)	☐	☐	☐

1 LISTENING *Celebrity interview*

A ▶ Listen to an interview with Jeri, a fashion model. Answer the questions.

1. Where did she grow up? ....
2. What did she want to do when she grew up? ....
3. Did she have a hobby? ....
4. Did she have a favorite game? ....
5. What was her favorite place? ....

B PAIR WORK Use the questions in part A to interview a partner about his or her childhood. Ask follow-up questions to get more information.

2 DISCUSSION *How times have changed!*

A PAIR WORK Talk about how life in your country has changed in the last 50 years. Ask questions like these:

How big were families 50 years ago?
What kinds of homes did people live in?
How did people use to dress?
How were schools different?
What kinds of jobs did men have? women?
How much did people use to earn?

A: How big were families 50 years ago?
B: Families used to be much larger. My grandfather had ten brothers and sisters!

B GROUP WORK Compare your answers. Do you think life was better in the old days? Why or why not?

3 SURVEY *City planner*

A What do you think about these things in your city or town? Complete the survey.

	Not enough	OK	Too many/Too much
places to go dancing	☐	☐	☐
places to listen to music	☐	☐	☐
noise	☐	☐	☐
places to sit and have coffee	☐	☐	☐
places to go shopping	☐	☐	☐
parking	☐	☐	☐
public transportation	☐	☐	☐
places to meet new people	☐	☐	☐

B **GROUP WORK** Compare your opinions and suggest ways to make your city or town better. Then agree on three improvements.

A: How would you make our city better?
B: There aren't enough places to go dancing. We need more nightclubs.
C: I disagree. There should be fewer clubs. There's too much noise downtown!

4 ROLE PLAY *Getting information*

Student A: Imagine you are a visitor in your city or town. Write five indirect questions about these categories. Then ask your questions to the hotel front-desk clerk.

Transportation   Hotels
Restaurants   Sightseeing
Shopping   Entertainment

Student B: You are a hotel front-desk clerk. Answer the guest's questions. Start like this: *Can I help you?*

Change roles and try the role play again.

useful expressions
Let me think. Oh, yes, . . .
I'm not really sure, but I think . . .
Sorry, I don't know.

WHAT'S NEXT?

Look at your Self-assessment again. Do you need to review anything?

3 Time for a change!

1 WORD POWER Houses and apartments

A These words are used to describe houses and apartments.
Which are positive (**P**)? Which are negative (**N**)?

bright

bright	...P....	dingy	....	private	....
comfortable	....	expensive	....	quiet	....
convenient	....	huge	....	safe	....
cramped	....	inconvenient	....	shabby	....
dangerous	....	modern	....	small	....
dark	....	noisy	....	spacious	....

B **PAIR WORK** Tell your partner two positive and two negative features
of your house or apartment.

"I live in a safe neighborhood, and my apartment is very bright.
However, it's very expensive and a little cramped."

2 PERSPECTIVES Which would you prefer?

A ▶ Listen to these opinions about houses
and apartments. Which ones are about space?

1. Apartments are too small for pets.
2. Apartments aren't big enough for families.
3. Apartments don't have as many rooms as houses.
4. Apartments have just as many expenses as houses.
5. Apartments don't have enough parking spaces.

6. Houses cost too much money.
7. Houses aren't as safe as apartments.
8. Houses aren't as convenient as apartments.
9. Houses don't have enough closet space.
10. Houses don't have as much privacy as apartments.

B **PAIR WORK** Look at the opinions again. Which
statements do you agree with?

A: I agree that apartments are too small for pets.
B: And they don't have enough parking spaces!

Evaluations and comparisons

Evaluations with adjectives
Apartments are**n't** big **enough** for families.
Apartments are **too** small for pets.

Evaluations with nouns
Apartments do**n't** have **enough** parking spaces.
Houses cost **too much** money.

Comparisons with adjectives
Houses are**n't as** convenient **as** apartments.
Houses are **just as** convenient **as** apartments.

Comparisons with nouns
Apartments have **just as many** rooms **as** houses.
Apartments do**n't** have **as much** privacy **as** houses.

A Imagine you are looking for a house or an apartment to rent. Read the two ads. Then rewrite the opinions below using the words in parentheses. Compare with a partner.

Spacious, modern house

3 bedrooms, 1 bathroom;
very private; in quiet
suburb; 2-car garage;
$1500 per month.

Smaller, older apartment

2 bedrooms, 1 bathroom;
downtown, near subway;
1 parking space;
$900 per month.

1. There are only a few windows. (not enough)
2. It's not bright enough. (too)
3. It has only one bathroom. (not enough)
4. It's not convenient enough. (too)

5. It's not spacious enough. (too)
6. It's too old. (not enough)
7. It isn't safe enough. (too)
8. There's only one parking space. (not enough)

There aren't enough windows.

B Write comparisons of the house and the apartment using these words and *as . . . as*. Then compare with a partner.

noisy	big
bedrooms	expensive
bathrooms	modern
spacious	convenient
private	parking spaces

The house isn't as noisy as the apartment.
The apartment doesn't have as many bedrooms as the house.

C **GROUP WORK** Which would you prefer to rent, the house or the apartment? Why?

A: I'd rent the apartment because the house costs too much.
B: I'd choose the house. The apartment isn't big enough for my family.

4 **PRONUNCIATION** *Unpronounced vowels*

A ▶ Listen and practice. The vowel immediately after a stressed syllable is sometimes not pronounced.

⬤ ○

av͟erage
diff͟erent
sep͟arate

⬤ ○ ○

comf͟ortable
int͟eresting
veg͟etable

B Write four sentences using some of the words in part A. Then read them with a partner. Pay attention to unpronounced vowels.

> In my hometown, the average apartment has two bedrooms.

5 **LISTENING** *Capsule hotels*

A ▶ Listen to Brad describe a "capsule hotel." Check (✓) the words that best describe it.

☐ cramped   ☐ convenient   ☐ bright
☐ expensive   ☐ busy   ☐ dangerous

B ▶ Listen again. In addition to a bed, what does the hotel provide? Write four things.

....
....

C **PAIR WORK** Would you like to stay in a capsule hotel? Why or why not?

6 **WRITING** *A descriptive email*

A Imagine you've just moved to this apartment. Write an email to a friend comparing your old home to your new one.

Dear Emma,

How are things with you? My big news is that I just moved to a new apartment! Do you remember my old apartment? It didn't have enough space. My new apartment has a huge living room and two bathrooms! Also, my old living room was too dark, but my new one is brighter. But there aren't enough windows in the bedrooms, so they're too dark. There are . . .

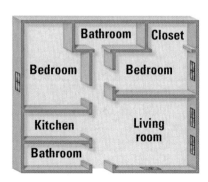

B **PAIR WORK** Read each other's emails. How are your descriptions similar? different?

7 SNAPSHOT

COMMON WISHES PEOPLE HAVE ABOUT THEIR LIVES

- ☐ IMPROVE MY PERSONALITY
- ☐ ENJOY LIFE MORE
- ☐ PLAY A MUSICAL INSTRUMENT
- ☐ FIND A BETTER JOB
- ☐ ADD MORE HOURS TO THE DAY
- ☐ GO BACK TO SCHOOL
- ☐ MOVE TO A NEW HOME
- ☐ MAKE SOME NEW FRIENDS
- ☐ SPEND MORE TIME WITH MY FAMILY

Source: Based on interviews with adults between the ages of 18 and 50

Check (✓) some of the things you would like to do. Then tell a partner why.
Which of these wishes would be easy to achieve? Which would be difficult or impossible?
What other things would you like to change about your life? Why?

8 CONVERSATION *Making changes*

A ▶ Listen and practice.

Brian: So, are you still living with your parents, Terry?

Terry: I'm afraid so. I wish I had my own apartment.

Brian: Why? Don't you like living at home?

Terry: It's OK, but my parents are always asking me to be home before midnight. I wish they'd stop worrying about me.

Brian: Yeah, parents are like that!

Terry: And they expect me to help around the house. I hate housework. I wish life weren't so difficult.

Brian: So, why don't you move out?

Terry: Hey, I wish I could, but where else can I get free room and board?

B ▶ Listen to the rest of the conversation. What changes would Brian like to make in his life?

9 GRAMMAR FOCUS

Wish ▶

Use wish + past tense to refer to present wishes.

I **live** with my parents.   Life **is** difficult.
    I wish I **didn't live** with my parents.   I wish it **were*** easier.
    I wish I **had** my own apartment.   I wish it **weren't** so difficult.
I **can't move** out.   My parents **won't stop** worrying about me.
    I wish I **could move** out.   I wish they **would stop** worrying about me.

*For the verb be, were is used with all pronouns after wish.

A Read these facts about people's lives. Then rewrite the sentences
using *wish*. (More than one answer is possible.)

1. Diane can't wear contact lenses.   *She wishes she could wear contact lenses.*
2. Beth's class is so boring.   *She wishes her class weren't so boring.*
3. My parents can't afford a new car.   ....
4. Dan can't fit into his old jeans.   ....
5. I can't remember my PIN number.   ....
6. Laura doesn't have any free time.   ....
7. Mitch is too short to play basketball.   ....

B PAIR WORK Think of five things you wish you could change.
Then discuss them with your partner.

A: What do you wish you could change?
B: Well, I'm not in very good shape. I wish I were more fit.

10 SPEAKING *Wish list*

A What do you wish were different about these
things? Write down your wishes.

my bedroom	my social life	my possessions
my school or job	my skills	my town

B GROUP WORK Compare your wishes. Does anyone
have the same wish?

A: I wish my bedroom were a different color. It's not bright enough.
B: Me, too! I wish I could paint my bedroom bright orange.
C: I like the color of my bedroom, but my bed is too small. I wish . . .

11 INTERCHANGE 3 *Wishful thinking*

Find out more about your classmates' wishes. Go to Interchange 3 on page 116.

Break those bad habits

Skim the article. What three bad habits does the article mention?

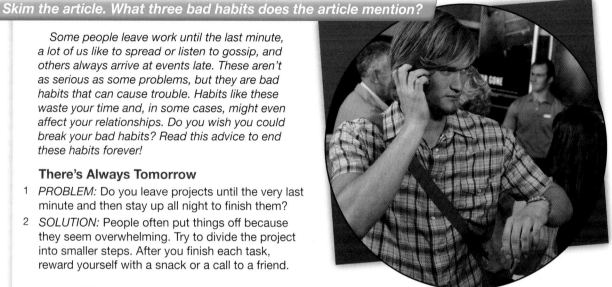

Some people leave work until the last minute, a lot of us like to spread or listen to gossip, and others always arrive at events late. These aren't as serious as some problems, but they are bad habits that can cause trouble. Habits like these waste your time and, in some cases, might even affect your relationships. Do you wish you could break your bad habits? Read this advice to end these habits forever!

There's Always Tomorrow

1 *PROBLEM:* Do you leave projects until the very last minute and then stay up all night to finish them?

2 *SOLUTION:* People often put things off because they seem overwhelming. Try to divide the project into smaller steps. After you finish each task, reward yourself with a snack or a call to a friend.

Guess What I Just Heard

3 *PROBLEM:* Do you think it's not nice to talk about other people, but do it anyway? Do you feel bad after you've done it?

4 *SOLUTION:* First, never listen to gossip. If someone tries to tell you a secret, just say, "Sorry. I'm not really interested." Then think of some other news to offer – about yourself.

Never on Time

5 *PROBLEM:* Are you always late? Do your friends invite you to events a half hour early?

6 *SOLUTION:* Use the reminder function in your phone. For example, if a movie starts at 8:00 and it takes you 20 minutes to get to the theater, you have to leave by 7:40. Put the event in your phone calendar, and then set it to send you a reminder at 7:30.

A Read the article. Then check (✓) the best description of the article.

☐ 1. The article starts with a description and then gives advice.
☐ 2. The article starts with a description and then gives facts.
☐ 3. The article gives the writer's opinion.

B Where do these sentences belong? Write the number of the paragraph where each sentence could go.

.... a. You can also ask a friend to come to your home before the event.
.... b. Ask yourself: "How would I feel if someone told my secrets?"
.... c. Do you ever make up excuses to explain your unfinished work?
.... d. Are you ever so late that the people you're meeting decide to leave?
.... e. You can also ask a friend to call you to ask about your progress.
.... f. Are people afraid to tell you things about themselves?

C **PAIR WORK** Discuss other ways to break each of these bad habits.

4 I've never heard of that!

1 SNAPSHOT

Favorite Ethnic Dishes

South Korea

Bulgogi

Beef marinated with soy sauce and other spices

Brazil

Feijoada

A dish made of black beans, garlic, spices, and meat

Morocco

Lamb Tagine

A stew of vegetables, lamb, fruit, and spices cooked in a clay dish

Singapore

Fish Head Curry

A dish made from a fish head cooked in a rich curry sauce

Sources: *Fodor's South America; Fodor's Southeast Asia;* www.globalgourmet.com

Which dishes are made with meat? with fish?
Have you ever tried any of these dishes? Which ones would you like to try?
What ethnic foods are popular in your country?

2 CONVERSATION *Have you ever . . . ?*

A ▶ Listen and practice.

Steve: Hey, this sounds strange – snails with garlic. Have you ever eaten snails?
Kathy: Yes, I have. I had them here just last week.
Steve: Did you like them?
Kathy: Yes, I did. They were delicious! Why don't you try some?
Steve: No, I don't think so.
Server: Have you decided on an appetizer yet?
Kathy: Yes. I'll have a small order of the snails, please.
Server: And you, sir?
Steve: I think I'll have the fried brains.
Kathy: Fried brains? I've never heard of that! It sounds scary.

B ▶ Listen to the rest of the conversation. How did Steve like the fried brains? What else did he order?

3 PRONUNCIATION Consonant clusters

A ▶ Listen and practice. Notice how the two consonants at the beginning of a word are pronounced together.

/k/	/t/	/m/	/n/	/p/	/r/	/l/
skim	start	smart	snack	spare	brown	blue
scan	step	smile	snow	speak	gray	play

B PAIR WORK Find one more word on page 22 for each consonant cluster in part A. Then practice saying the words.

4 GRAMMAR FOCUS

Simple past vs. present perfect ▶

Use the simple past for experiences at a definite time in the past.
Use the present perfect for experiences within a time period up to the present.

Have you ever **eaten** snails?
   Yes, I **have**. I **tried** them last month.
Did you **like** them?
   Yes, I **did**. They **were** delicious.

Have you ever **been** to a Vietnamese restaurant?
   No, I **haven't**. But I **ate** at a Thai restaurant last night.
Did you **go** alone?
   No, I **went** with some friends.

A Complete these conversations. Then practice with a partner.

1. A: Have you ever ....._been_..... (be) to a picnic at the beach?
   B: Yes, I .... My family and I .... (have) a picnic on the beach last month. We .... (cook) hamburgers.

2. A: Have you ever .... (try) sushi?
   B: No, I .... , but I'd like to.

3. A: Did you .... (have) breakfast today?
   B: Yes, I .... I .... (eat) a huge breakfast.

4. A: Have you ever .... (eat) Mexican food?
   B: Yes, I .... In fact, I .... (eat) some just last week.

5. A: Did you .... (drink) coffee this morning?
   B: Yes, I .... I .... (have) some on my way to work.

B PAIR WORK Ask and answer the questions in part A. Give your own information.

5 LISTENING What are they talking about?

▶ Listen to six people ask questions about food and drink in a restaurant. Check (✓) the item that each person is talking about.

1. ☐ water   2. ☐ a meal   3. ☐ soup   4. ☐ coffee   5. ☐ cake   6. ☐ the check
   ☐ bread   ☐ a plate   ☐ pasta   ☐ meat   ☐ coffee   ☐ the menu

SPEAKING *Tell me more!*

PAIR WORK Ask your partner these questions and four more of your own. Then ask follow-up questions.

Have you ever drunk fresh coconut juice?
Have you ever been to a vegetarian restaurant?
Have you ever had an unusual ice-cream flavor?
Have you ever eaten something you didn't like?

A: Have you ever drunk fresh coconut juice?
B: Yes, I have.
A: Did you like it?
B: Yes, I did. Actually, I ordered a second one!

 7

INTERCHANGE 4 *Is that so?*

Find out some interesting facts about your classmates. Go to Interchange 4 on page 117.

8 WORD POWER *Cooking methods*

A How do you cook the foods below? Check (✓) the methods that are most common in your country. Then compare with a partner.

bake	**boil**	**fry**	**grill**	**roast**	**steam**

Methods	Foods								
	fish	shrimp	eggs	chicken	beef	potatoes	onions	eggplant	bananas
bake	☐	☐	☐	☐	☐	☐	☐	☐	☐
boil	☐	☐	☐	☐	☐	☐	☐	☐	☐
fry	☐	☐	☐	☐	☐	☐	☐	☐	☐
grill	☐	☐	☐	☐	☐	☐	☐	☐	☐
roast	☐	☐	☐	☐	☐	☐	☐	☐	☐
steam	☐	☐	☐	☐	☐	☐	☐	☐	☐

B PAIR WORK What's your favorite way to cook or eat the foods in part A?

A: Have you ever steamed fish?
B: No, I haven't. I prefer to bake it.

9 PERSPECTIVES *Family cookbook*

A ▶ Listen to this recipe for Elvis Presley's favorite sandwich. Do you think this is a healthy snack?

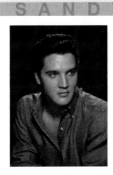

S A N D W I C H E S

Peanut butter and banana

3 tablespoons peanut butter
1 banana, mashed
2 slices of bread
2 tablespoons butter, melted

First, mix the peanut butter and mashed banana together. Then lightly toast the slices of bread. Next, spread the peanut butter and banana mixture on the toast.

After that, close the sandwich and put it in a pan with melted butter. Finally, fry the bread until it's brown on both sides.

S A N D W I C H E S

B PAIR WORK Look at the steps in the recipe again. Number the pictures from 1 to 5. Would you like to try Elvis's specialty?

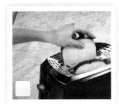    

10 GRAMMAR FOCUS

> ### Sequence adverbs ▶
>
> **First**, mix the peanut butter and banana together.
> **Then** toast the slices of bread.
> **Next**, spread the mixture on the toast.
> **After that**, put the sandwich in a pan with butter.
> **Finally**, fry the sandwich until it's brown on both sides.

A Here's a recipe for grilled kebabs. Look at the pictures and number the steps from 1 to 5. Then add a sequence adverb to each step.

☐ .... put the meat and vegetables on the skewers.
1 ...First... put charcoal in the grill and light it.
☐ .... take the kebabs off the grill and enjoy!
☐ .... put the kebabs on the grill and cook for 10 to 15 minutes, turning them over from time to time.
☐ .... cut up some meat and vegetables. Marinate them for 20 minutes in your favorite sauce.

B PAIR WORK Cover the recipe and look only at the pictures. Explain each step of the recipe to your partner.

11 LISTENING Tempting snacks

A Listen to people explain how to make these snacks. Which snack are they talking about? Number the photos from 1 to 4. (There is one extra photo.)

a bagel **cookies** **guacamole** **pizza** **popcorn**

B **PAIR WORK** Choose one of the snacks you just heard about. Tell your partner how to make it.

12 SPEAKING My favorite snack

GROUP WORK Discuss these questions.

What's your favorite snack?
Is it easy to make?
What's in it?
When do you eat it?
How often do you eat it?
How healthy is it?

"My favorite snack is ramen. It's very easy to make. First, . . ."

13 WRITING A recipe

A Read this recipe. Is this an easy recipe to make?

Spicy Salsa

half an onion   2 chili peppers
5 tomatoes   a small bunch of cilantro
salt and pepper   1 lemon

First, chop the onion, chili peppers, tomatoes, and cilantro. Put in a bowl. Next, add salt and pepper. Then squeeze some fresh lemon juice in the bowl. After that, mix everything together and refrigerate for one hour. Enjoy with tortilla chips.

B Now think of something you know how to make. First, write down the things you need. Then describe how to make it.

C **GROUP WORK** Read and discuss each recipe. Then choose one to share with the class. Explain why you chose it.

FOOD & MOOD

Follow   Share 5

Skim the article. Then check (✓) the main idea.
☐ *Certain foods cause stress and depression.* ☐ *Certain foods affect the way we feel.*

We often eat to calm down or cheer up when we're feeling stressed or depressed. Now new research suggests there's a reason: Food changes our brain chemistry. These changes powerfully influence our moods. But can certain foods really make us feel better? Nutrition experts say yes. But what should we eat, and what should we avoid? Here are the foods that work the best, as well as those that can make a bad day worse.

To Outsmart Stress

What's good? Recent research suggests that foods that are high in carbohydrates, such as bread, rice, and pasta, can help you calm down. Researchers say that carbohydrates cause the brain to release a chemical called serotonin. Serotonin makes you feel better.

What's bad? Many people drink coffee when they feel stress. The warmth is soothing, and the caffeine in coffee might help you think more clearly. But if you drink too much, you may become even more anxious and irritable.

To Soothe the Blues

What's good? Introduce more lean meat, chicken, seafood, and whole grains into your diet. These foods have a lot of selenium. Selenium is a mineral that helps people feel more relaxed and happy. You can also try eating a Brazil nut every day. One Brazil nut contains a lot of selenium.

What's bad? When they're feeling low, many people turn to comfort foods – or foods that make them feel happy or secure. These often include things like sweet desserts. A chocolate bar may make you feel better at first, but within an hour you may feel worse than you did before.

A Read the article. The sentences below are false. Correct each sentence to make it true.

1. We often eat when we feel calm.
2. You should drink coffee to relieve stress.
3. Foods like chicken and seafood are high in carbohydrates.
4. Carbohydrates cause the brain to release selenium.
5. Serotonin makes you feel more anxious and irritable.
6. People usually eat comfort foods when they're feeling happy.
7. Brazil nuts don't contain much selenium.
8. Chocolate will make you feel better.

B **PAIR WORK** What foods do you eat to feel better? After reading the article, which of the suggestions will you follow?

Units 3–4 Progress check

SELF-ASSESSMENT

How well can you do these things? Check (✓) the boxes.

I can	Very well	OK	A little
Describe a house or an apartment (Ex. 1)	☐	☐	☐
Express opinions about houses or apartments; agree and disagree (Ex. 1)	☐	☐	☐
Understand and express personal wishes (Ex. 2)	☐	☐	☐
Ask and answer questions about past actions and personal experiences (Ex. 3)	☐	☐	☐
Describe recipes (Ex. 4)	☐	☐	☐

1 SPEAKING *Apartment ads*

A **PAIR WORK** Use the topics in the box to write an ad for an apartment.
Use this ad as a model. Make the apartment sound as good as possible.

Quiet, Private Apartment
Small, but very comfortable, with many windows;
located downtown; convenient to stores; 1 bedroom,
1 bathroom; 1-car garage; $850 a month!

age	windows	parking
size	bathroom(s)	cost
location	bedroom(s)	noise

B **GROUP WORK** Join another pair. Evaluate and compare the apartments.
Which would you prefer to rent? Why?

A: There aren't enough bedrooms in your apartment.
B: But it's convenient.
C: Yes, but our apartment is just as convenient!

2 LISTENING *I really need a change!*

A ▶ Listen to three people talk about things they wish they could change.
Check (✓) the topic each person is talking about.

1. ☐ free time   ☐ school   ....
2. ☐ skills   ☐ hobbies ....
3. ☐ family   ☐ travel   ....

B ▶ Listen again. Write one change each person would like to make.

C **GROUP WORK** Use the topics in part A to express some wishes.
How can you make the wishes come true? Offer suggestions.

3 SURVEY *Food experiences*

A Complete the survey with your food opinions and experiences. Then use your information to write questions.

Me	Name
1. I've eaten .... I liked it. _Have you ever eaten_ .... _? Did you like it?_	....
2. I've eaten .... I hated it. ....? ....?	....
3. I've never tried .... But I want to.	....
4. I've been to the restaurant .... I enjoyed it.	....
5. I've made .... for my friends. They loved it.	....

B **CLASS ACTIVITY** Go around the class and ask your questions. Find people who have the same opinions and experiences. Write a classmate's name only once.

A: Have you ever eaten peanut butter?
B: Yes, I have.
A: Did you like it?
B: No, not really.

4 ROLE PLAY Iron Chef

GROUP WORK Work in groups of four. Two students are the judges. Two students are the chefs.

Judges: Make a list of three ingredients for the chefs to use. You will decide which chef creates the best recipe.

Chefs: Think of a recipe using the three ingredients the judges give you and other basic ingredients. Name the recipe and describe how to make it.

"My recipe is called . . . . To make it, first . . . . Then . . . . Next, . . . "

Change roles and try the role play again.

Iron Chef, a TV cooking competition

WHAT'S NEXT?

Look at your Self-assessment again. Do you need to review anything?

5 Going places

1 SNAPSHOT

What do you like to do on vacation?

Take a fun trip	Discover something new	Stay home	Enjoy nature

- travel in my country
- visit a foreign country
- visit museums
- go to a music festival
- hang out with friends
- watch movies
- go fishing
- relax at the beach

Source: Based on information from *U.S. News and World Report; American Demographics*

Which activities do you like to do on vacation? Check (✓) the activities.
Which activities did you do on your last vacation?
Make a list of other activities you like to do on vacation. Then compare with a partner.

2 CONVERSATION *What are you going to do?*

A ▶ Listen and practice.

Julia: I'm so excited! We have two weeks off!
What are you going to do?

Nancy: I'm not sure. I guess I'll just stay home.
Maybe I'll hang out with my friends and watch
some movies. What about you? Any plans?

Julia: Yeah, I'm going to relax at the beach with my
cousin. We're going to go surfing every day.
And my cousin likes to fish, so maybe
we'll go fishing one day.

Nancy: Sounds like fun.

Julia: Say, why don't you come with us?

Nancy: Do you mean it? I'd love to! I'll bring my surfboard!

Julia: That's great! The more the merrier!

B ▶ Listen to the rest of the conversation. Where
are they going to stay? How will they get there?

Future with be going to *and* will ▶

Use be going to + verb for plans you've decided on.	**Use will + verb for possible plans before you've made a decision.**
What **are** you **going to do**?	What **are** you **going to do**?
I'm going to relax at the beach.	I'm not sure. I **guess** I**'ll** just **stay** home.
We**'re going to go** surfing every day.	**Maybe** I**'ll watch** some movies.
I**'m** not **going to do** anything special.	I don't know. I **think** I**'ll go** camping.
	I **probably won't go** anywhere.

A Complete the conversation with appropriate forms of
be going to or *will*. Then compare with a partner.

A: Have you made any vacation plans?
B: Well, I've decided on one thing –
   I .... go camping.
A: That's great! For how long?
B: I .... be away for a week.
   I only have five days of vacation.
A: So, when are you leaving?
B: I'm not sure. I .... probably leave
   around the end of May.
A: And where .... you .... go?
B: I haven't thought about that yet. I guess
   I .... go to one of the national parks.
A: That sounds like fun.
B: Yeah. Maybe I .... go
   hiking and do some fishing.
A: .... you .... rent a camper?
B: I'm not sure. Actually, I probably ....
   rent a camper – it's too expensive.
A: .... you .... go with anyone?
B: No. I need some time alone.
   I .... travel by myself.

B Have you thought about your next vacation? Write answers to these
questions. (If you already have plans, use *be going to*. If you don't have
fixed plans, use *will*.)

1. How are you going to spend your next vacation?
2. Where are you going to go?
3. When are you going to take your vacation?
4. How long are you going to be on vacation?
5. Is anyone going to travel with you?

> I'm going to spend my next vacation . . .
> OR
> I'm not sure. Maybe I'll . . .

C **GROUP WORK** Take turns telling the group about your vacation plans.
Use your information from part B.

4 WORD POWER *Travel planning*

A Complete the chart. Then add one more word to each category.

ATM card	cash	hiking boots	plane ticket	suitcase
backpack	credit card	medication	sandals	swimsuit
carry-on bag	first-aid kit	passport	student ID	vaccination

Clothing	Money	Health	Documents	Luggage

B **PAIR WORK** What are the five most important items you need for these vacations?

a hiking trip   a rafting trip   a trip to a foreign country

 5 INTERCHANGE 5 *Fun vacations*

Decide between two vacations. Student A, go to Interchange 5A on page 118;
Student B, go to Interchange 5B on page 120.

 6 PERSPECTIVES *Travel advice*

A ▶ Listen to these pieces of advice from experienced travelers.
What topic is each person talking about?

"You should tell the driver where you're going before you get on. And you have to have exact change for the fare."

"In most countries, you don't have to have an international driver's license, but you must have a license from your own country. You also need to be 21 or over."

"You should try some of the local specialties, but you'd better avoid the stalls on the street."

"You ought to pack a first-aid kit and any medication you need. You shouldn't drink water from the tap."

"When you fly, you should keep important things in your carry-on bag, such as your medication and credit cards. You shouldn't pack them in your checked luggage."

"You ought to keep a copy of your credit card numbers at the hotel. And you shouldn't carry a lot of cash when you go out."

B **PAIR WORK** Look at the advice again. Do you think this is all good advice? Why or why not?

GRAMMAR FOCUS

Modals for necessity and suggestion ⊙

Describing necessity
You **must** have a driver's license.
You **need to** be 21 or over.
You **have to** get a passport.
You **don't have to** get vaccinations.

Giving suggestions
You**'d better** avoid the stalls on the street.
You **ought to** pack a first-aid kit.
You **should** try some local specialties.
You **shouldn't** carry a lot of cash.

A Choose the best advice for someone who is going on vacation. Then compare with a partner.

1. You .... make hotel reservations in advance. It might be difficult to find a room after you get there. (have to / 'd better)
2. You .... carry identification with you. It's the law! (must / should)
3. You .... buy a round-trip plane ticket because it's cheaper. (must / should)
4. You .... pack too many clothes. You won't have room to bring back any gifts. (don't have to / shouldn't)
5. You .... check out of most hotel rooms by noon if you don't want to pay for another night. (need to / ought to)
6. You .... buy a new suitcase because your old one is getting shabby. (have to / ought to)

B **PAIR WORK** Imagine you're going to travel abroad. Take turns giving each other advice.

"You must get the necessary vaccinations."

1. You . . . get the necessary vaccinations.
2. You . . . take your ATM card with you.
3. You . . . take your student ID. It might get you discounts.
4. You . . . forget to pack your camera.
5. You . . . have a visa to enter some foreign countries.
6. You . . . change money before you go. You can do it when you arrive.

C **GROUP WORK** What advice would you give someone who is going to study English abroad? Report your best ideas to the class.

PRONUNCIATION *Linked sounds with /w/ and /y/*

⊙ Listen and practice. Notice how some words are linked by a /w/ sound, and other words are linked by a /y/ sound.

/w/
You should know about local conditions.

/y/
You shouldn't carry a lot of cash.

/w/
You ought to do it right away.

/y/
You must be at least 21 years old.

9 LISTENING Tourist tips

A ▶ Listen to an interview with a spokeswoman from the New York City Visitors Center. Check (✓) the four topics she discusses.

☐ eating out   ☐ history   ☐ money   ☐ planning a trip   ☐ safety   ☐ tours

B ▶ Listen again. For each topic, write one piece of advice she gives.

10 WRITING Travel suggestions

A Imagine someone is going to visit your town, city, or country. Write a letter giving some suggestions for sightseeing activities.

> Dear Josh,
>
> I'm so glad you're going to visit Santiago! As you know, Santiago is a very old and beautiful city, so you should bring your camera. Also, you ought to bring some good shoes because we're going to walk a lot. It will be warm, so you don't have to pack . . .

B **PAIR WORK** Exchange letters. Is there anything else the visitor needs to know about (food, money, business hours, etc.)?

11 DISCUSSION Dream vacation

A **PAIR WORK** You just won a free 30-day trip around the world. Discuss the following questions.

When will you leave and return?
Which direction will you go (east or west)?
Where will you choose to stop? Why?
How will you get from place to place?
How long will you stay in each place?

B **PAIR WORK** What do you need to do before you go? Discuss these topics.

| reservations | documents | vaccinations |
| money | shopping | packing |

A: We should make a hotel reservation for the first night.
B: Yes, and I think we ought to buy some guidebooks.

Volunteer Travel – A vacation with a difference

Check (✓) the statements you think are true. Then scan the article to check your answers.
- ☐ Volunteer travelers don't receive money for their work.
- ☐ Volunteer travel is only for young people.

For her vacation each year, Allie Lebrun goes volunteer traveling. In a recent interview with *Volunteer Magazine*, she talked about volunteer vacations.

VM: --

AL: It's like an exchange program. People find a program in a country they'd like to visit. In exchange for food and accommodations, they work. In other words, they don't get a salary. The idea is that volunteers can learn about real people in other countries. Vacationers who stay in hotels often don't learn much about the local people and culture.

VM: --

AL: Many of the jobs are on small farms. Farmers often need volunteers to harvest crops. I've harvested vegetables and fruit – including nuts and olives! Some volunteers work with animals, such as milking cows or goats. That's an interesting experience, I can tell you! And sometimes farmers want volunteers to do things like build stone walls. There are lots of possibilities.

VM: --

AL: Anyone! Many volunteers are fairly young. The work can be hard, so a volunteer needs to be fit. But, actually, age isn't important. I've worked with people in their seventies and even eighties!

VM: --

AL: Just about anywhere in the world! I've volunteered in Italy, Morocco, Indonesia, and several countries in Latin America.

VM: --

AL: Oh, that's easy! Just go online. Do a search for "volunteer travel" or "volunteer vacations." You'll find lots of websites with information about opportunities for volunteering. Maybe there's a program in a country you've always wanted to visit!

A Read the article. Then write these questions in the appropriate place.

1. What kinds of work can volunteers do?
2. Where can people volunteer to work?
3. Who can volunteer?
4. And finally, how can someone find out about volunteer travel opportunities?
5. What is volunteer traveling?

B Complete the summary with information from the article.

Allie Lebrun goes .... every year. She says that volunteers get .... in exchange for .... Volunteers often work on ....
and harvest .... To volunteer, you have to be fit, but age .... You
can work .... in the world. To find places to work, ... There are
.... with information about volunteer traveling.

C **GROUP WORK** Would you like to volunteer travel? Where would you like to go?
What kind of work would you like to do? Why?

6 OK. No problem!

1 **SNAPSHOT**

MY KIDS...
- ☐ don't help around the house
- ☐ are always texting their friends
- ☐ never listen to us
- ☐ eat too much junk food
- ☐ leave everything until the last minute

Common Complaints of Families with Teenagers

MY PARENTS...
- ☐ embarrass me in front of my friends
- ☐ don't respect my privacy
- ☐ criticize my taste in music
- ☐ nag me to clean up my room
- ☐ won't let me make my own decisions

Sources: Based on interviews with parents and teenagers

Which complaints seem reasonable? Which ones seem unreasonable? Why?
Check (✓) a complaint you have about a family member.
What other complaints do people sometimes have about family members?

2 **CONVERSATION** *Turn down the TV!*

A ▶ Listen and practice.

Mr. Field: Jason . . . Jason! Turn down the TV, please.
    Jason: Oh, but this is my favorite program!
Mr. Field: I know. But it's very loud.
    Jason: OK. I'll turn it down.
Mr. Field: That's better. Thanks.
Mrs. Field: Lisa, please pick up your things.
              They're all over the floor.
     Lisa: In a minute, Mom. I'm on the phone.
Mrs. Field: All right. But do it as soon as you hang up.
     Lisa: OK. No problem!
Mrs. Field: Were we like this when we were kids?
 Mr. Field: Definitely!

B ▶ Listen to the rest of the conversation.
What complaints do Jason and Lisa have
about their parents?

3 GRAMMAR FOCUS

Two-part verbs; will *for responding to requests* ▶

With nouns	**With pronouns**	**Requests and responses**
Turn down the TV.	**Turn it** down.	Please turn down the music.
Turn the TV **down**.	(NOT: ~~Turn down it.~~)	OK. I**'ll** turn it down.
Pick up your things.	**Pick** them **up**.	Pick up your clothes, please.
Pick your things **up**.	(NOT: ~~Pick up them.~~)	All right. I**'ll** pick them up.

A Complete the requests with these words. Then compare with a partner.

the books

the toys

the music

your jacket

the TV

your boots

the yard

the lights

the trash

the cat

1. Pick up ....the toys............ , please.
2. Turn .... off, please.
3. Clean .... up, please.
4. Please put .... away.
5. Please turn down ....

6. Please take off ....
7. Hang .... up, please.
8. Please take out ....
9. Please let .... out.
10. Turn on .... , please.

B **PAIR WORK** Take turns making the requests above. Respond with pronouns.

A: Pick up the toys, please.
B: No problem. I'll pick them up.

4 PRONUNCIATION *Stress in two-part verbs*

A ▶ Listen and practice. Both words in a two-part verb receive equal stress.

● ● ○ ●   ● ○ ● ●   ● ○ ●
Pick up the toys.   Pick the toys up.   Pick them up.
Turn off the light.   Turn the light off.   Turn it off.

B Write four more requests using the verbs in Exercise 3.
Then practice with a partner. Pay attention to stress.

5 WORD POWER Household chores

A Find a phrase that is usually paired with each two-part verb. (Some phrases go with more than one verb.) Then add one more phrase for each verb.

the garbage   the magazines   the microwave   your coat
the groceries   the mess   the towels   your laptop

clean up	....	....	take out	....	....
hang up	....	....	throw out	....	....
pick up	....	....	turn off	....	....
put away	....	....	turn on	....	....

B What requests can you make in each of these rooms? Write four requests and four excuses. Use two-part verbs.

the kitchen   the living room
the bathroom   the bedroom

C PAIR WORK Take turns making the requests you wrote in part B. Respond by giving an excuse.

A: Kim, please hang up the coat you left in the living room.
B: Sorry, I can't hang it up right now. I need to take the cat out for a walk.

6 LISTENING Family life

A ⊙ Listen to the results of a survey about family life. Answer each question with men (**M**), women (**W**), boys (**B**), or girls (**G**).

Who is the messiest person in the house? ....
Who does most of the work in the kitchen? ....
Who usually takes out the garbage? ....
Who worries most about expenses? ....

B ⊙ Listen again. According to the survey, what specific chores do men, women, boys, and girls usually do? Take notes.

C GROUP WORK Discuss the questions in parts A and B. Who does these things in your family?

7 PERSPECTIVES *Reasonable requests?*

A ⊙ Match the sentences. Then listen and check your answers.
Are all the requests reasonable?

1. "Could you please tell me the next time you have a party? ....

2. "Can you turn the music down, please? ....

3. "Would you mind closing the door behind you and making sure it locks? ....

4. "Would you please tell your guests to use the visitor parking spaces? ....

5. "Would you mind not putting your garbage in the hallway? ....

a. It's not very pleasant to see when I walk by."

b. We don't want strangers to enter the building."

c. The walls are really thin, so the sound goes through to my apartment."

d. A lot of cars have been using my space recently."

e. I'd like to make sure I'm not at home."

B Look at the requests again. Have you ever made similar requests?
Has anyone ever asked you to do similar things?

8 GRAMMAR FOCUS

> ## Requests with modals and Would you mind . . . ? ⊙
>
> **Modal + simple form of verb**
> **Can** you **turn** the music **down**?
> **Could** you **close** the door, please?
> **Would** you please **take** your garbage **out**?
>
> **Would you mind . . . + gerund**
> **Would you mind turning** the music **down**?
> **Would you mind closing** the door, please?
> **Would you mind not putting** your garbage here?

A Match the requests in column A with the appropriate responses in column B. Then compare
with a partner and practice them. (More than one answer may be possible.)

A
1. Could you lend me twenty dollars? ....
2. Can you make me a sandwich? ....
3. Can you help me with my homework? ....
4. Would you mind not sitting here? ....
5. Would you please turn down the TV? ....
6. Would you mind speaking more quietly? ....

B
a. Sorry. We didn't know we were so loud.
b. Sure. Do you want anything to drink?
c. Sorry. I didn't realize this seat was taken.
d. I'm sorry, I can't. I don't have any cash.
e. I'm really sorry, but I'm busy.
f. Sure, no problem. I'd be glad to.

B PAIR WORK Take turns making the requests in part A. Give your own responses.

C CLASS ACTIVITY Think of five unusual requests. Go around the class and
make your requests. How many people accept? How many refuse?

A: Would you please sing a song for me?
B: Oh, I'm sorry. I'm a terrible singer.

9 SPEAKING Apologies

A Think of three complaints you have about your neighbors. Write three requests you want to make. Choose from these topics or use ideas of your own.

garbage   guests   noise   parking   pets   security

B **PAIR WORK** Take turns making your requests. The "neighbor" should apologize by giving an excuse, admitting a mistake, or making an offer or a promise.

A: Would you mind not putting your garbage in the hallway?
B: Oh, I'm sorry. I didn't realize it bothered you.

different ways to apologize	
give an excuse	"I'm sorry. I didn't realize . . ."
admit a mistake	"I forgot I left it there."
make an offer	"I'll take it out right now."
make a promise	"I promise I'll . . . / I'll make sure to . . ."

10 INTERCHANGE 6 That's no excuse!

How good are you at apologizing? Go to Interchange 6 on page 119.

11 WRITING A set of guidelines

A **PAIR WORK** Imagine that you live in a large apartment building. Use complaints from Exercise 9 and your own ideas to write a set of six guidelines.

The Riverview Apartments

Please read the following tenant association guidelines. Feel free to contact Joseph (#205) or Tina (#634) if you have any questions.

1. Don't park bicycles on the sidewalk. Everyone must use the bike rack.

2. Can everyone please keep the laundry room clean? Please pick up after yourself!

3. Would you mind not picking the flowers in the garden? They're for everyone's enjoyment.

B **GROUP WORK** Take turns reading your guidelines aloud. What is the best new guideline? the worst one?

How to Ask for a Favor

Read the headings in the article. Can you think of other good advice when asking for a favor?

We all have to ask for favors sometimes. But it can be a difficult thing to do – even when you ask a good friend. So how can you ask a favor and be reasonably sure to get a positive response? Here are some suggestions.

Mike, would you mind doing me a favor?

Choose your words carefully

How do people respond to requests like this one: "Hey, Mike, lend me your car!"? They probably refuse. How can you avoid this problem? Choose your words carefully! For example, say, "Mike, would you mind doing me a favor?" Mike will probably respond like this: "Maybe. What do you need?" Now you have his attention and can explain the situation. People are more likely to agree to help you when they know the whole story.

Be a nice person

When you ask someone for a favor, you're really asking the person to go out of his or her way to help you. Show the person that you understand he or she is doing something *especially* nice for you. If people think you're *pleasant*, they're more likely to want to help. Thank them *sincerely* when they help you. And, of course, a smile goes a long way.

Give and take

If someone agrees to do you a favor, allow the person to choose when he or she helps you. Be respectful of the other person's time, and try not to ask for too much. If someone *refuses* your request, you should accept the answer politely. Don't make a habit of asking for favors, and always make sure you're ready to do someone a favor in return. *Reciprocate.* It's just a matter of giving and taking.

A Read the article. Find the words in *italics* below in the article. Then match each word with its meaning.

.... 1. *especially*   a. give in return
.... 2. *pleasant*   b. say no
.... 3. *sincerely*   c. friendly
.... 4. *refuse*   d. more than usually
.... 5. *avoid*   e. honestly
.... 6. *reciprocate*   f. stop from happening

B Check (✓) the questions that the article answers. Then find sentences in the article that support your answers.

☐ 1. Why is it easy to ask for a favor?
☐ 2. How can you show people you're nice?
☐ 3. How can you avoid people asking for favors?

☐ 4. What do you do when someone refuses?
☐ 5. Why is it not a good idea to ask for a lot of favors?

C **PAIR WORK** Think about a favor you asked someone to do. Did the person do it? Then think about a favor someone asked you to do. Did you do it? Why or why not?

Units 5–6 Progress check

SELF-ASSESSMENT

How well can you do these things? Check (✓) the boxes.

I can	Very well	OK	A little
Understand descriptions of people's plans (Ex. 1)	☐	☐	☐
Ask and answer questions about personal plans (Ex. 2)	☐	☐	☐
Give travel advice (Ex. 2)	☐	☐	☐
Make and respond to practical requests (Ex. 3, 4)	☐	☐	☐
Apologize and give excuses (Ex. 3, 4)	☐	☐	☐

 1 LISTENING *Summer plans*

A ⏵ Listen to Judy, Paul, and Brenda describe their summer plans.
What is each person going to do?

	Summer plans	Reason
1. Judy	....	....
2. Paul	....	....
3. Brenda	....	....

B ⏵ Listen again. What is the reason for each person's choice?

2 DISCUSSION *Planning a vacation*

A GROUP WORK Imagine you are going to go on vacation.
Take turns asking and answering these questions.

A: **Where are you going to go on your next vacation?**
B: I'm going to go to Utah.
A: **What are you going to do?**
B: I'm going to go camping and hiking.
Maybe I'll try rock climbing.
A: **Why did you choose that?**
B: Well, I really enjoy nature. And I want to do
something different!

B GROUP WORK What should each person do to prepare
for his or her vacation? Give each other advice.

3 ROLE PLAY *Excuses, excuses!*

Student A: Your partner was supposed to do some things, but didn't. Look at the pictures and make a request about each one.

Student B: You were supposed to do some things, but didn't. Listen to your partner's requests. Apologize and either agree to the request or give an excuse.

A: You left the towels on the floor. Please hang them up.
B: I'm sorry. I forgot about them. I'll hang them up right now.

Change roles and try the role play again.

4 GAME *Could you do me a favor?*

A Write three requests on separate cards. Put an *X* on the back of two of the cards.

| Can you cook dinner tonight? | Could you get me a cup of coffee? | Would you mind closing the window? |

B CLASS ACTIVITY Shuffle all the cards together. Take three new cards.

Go around the class and take turns making requests with the cards. Hold up each card so your classmate can see the back.

When answering:
X on the back = refuse the request and give an excuse
No *X* = agree to the request

Can you cook dinner tonight?

I'm sorry, I can't. I'm . . .

WHAT'S NEXT?

Look at your Self-assessment again. Do you need to review anything?

7 What's this for?

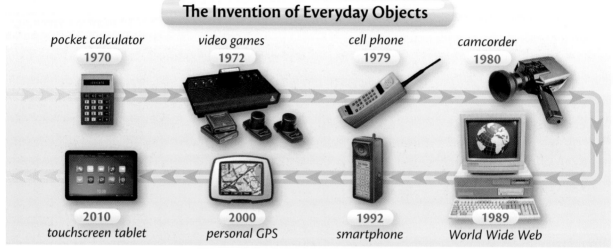

The Invention of Everyday Objects

| pocket calculator | video games | cell phone | camcorder |
| 1970 | 1972 | 1979 | 1980 |

| 2010 | 2000 | 1992 | 1989 |
| touchscreen tablet | personal GPS | smartphone | World Wide Web |

Sources: *The People's Almanac Presents the 20th Century;* www.about.com; www.ehow.com

Circle the things that you use every day or almost every day.
Which invention do you think is the most important? the least important?
What are some other things you use every day?

2 PERSPECTIVES *Computer usage*

A ▶ How do you use a computer? Listen and respond to the statements.

Rate Your Computer Usage

I use a computer . . .	Often	Sometimes	Hardly ever	Never
to send emails	☐	☐	☐	☐
for watching movies	☐	☐	☐	☐
to play games	☐	☐	☐	☐
to shop online	☐	☐	☐	☐
for doing school assignments	☐	☐	☐	☐
to learn languages	☐	☐	☐	☐
for video chatting	☐	☐	☐	☐
to check the weather	☐	☐	☐	☐
to read the news	☐	☐	☐	☐
for downloading music	☐	☐	☐	☐

B PAIR WORK Compare your answers. Are your answers similar or different?

> **Infinitives and gerunds for uses and purposes** ▶
>
> | Infinitives | Gerunds |
> |---|---|
> | I use my computer **to send** emails. | I use my computer **for sending** emails. |
> | Some people use computers **to play** games. | Some people use computers **for playing** games. |
> | Computers are often used **to watch** movies. | Computers are often used **for watching** movies. |

A **PAIR WORK** What do you know about this technology? Complete the sentences in column A with information from column B. Use infinitives and gerunds. (More than one combination is possible.)

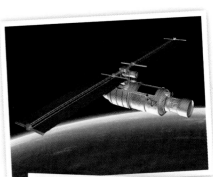

A

1. Satellites are used . . .
2. Robots are sometimes used . . .
3. You can use a cell phone . . .
4. People use the Internet . . .
5. A GPS device is used . . .
6. A tablet computer can be used . . .

B

study the world's weather
perform dangerous tasks
read e-books
transmit telephone calls
send text messages
get directions
make travel reservations
transmit TV shows
shop online

> Satellites are used to study the world's weather.
> Satellites are used for studying the world's weather.

B **GROUP WORK** Think of three more items of technology. Then talk about possible uses for each one.

"You can use an MP3 player to listen to podcasts."

4 *PRONUNCIATION* *Syllable stress*

A ▶ Listen and practice. Notice which syllable has the main stress.

●ₒₒ	ₒ●ₒ	ₒₒ●
satellite	invention	CD-ROM
Internet	assignment	engineer
messages	computer	entertain
....	....	....
....	....	....

B ▶ Where is the stress in these words? Add them to the columns in part A. Then listen and check.

directions   DVD   media   telephone   transmission   understand

5 WORD POWER *The world of computers*

A Complete the chart with words and phrases from the list. Add one more to each category. Then compare with a partner.

- ✓ browse websites
- computer whiz
- create a slideshow
- create song playlists
- cut and paste
- drag and drop
- edit a video
- flash drive
- geek
- hacker
- highlight text
- keyboard
- monitor
- mouse
- open a file
- technophile

People who are "into" computers	Type of computer hardware	Fun things to do with a computer	Things to do with a mouse
		browse websites	

B **GROUP WORK** Discuss how computers have changed our lives. Ask and answer questions like these:

How do computers make your life easier? more difficult?
How do they affect the way you spend your free time?
How do they influence the kinds of jobs people have?
What kinds of problems do they cause?
Do you know anyone who is a computer whiz?
Are hackers a problem where you live?

6 LISTENING *Off-line – and proud of it!*

A Guess the answers to the questions below. Then listen to a radio program about the Internet and check your answers.

What percentage of the U.S. population never uses the Internet? What kinds of people don't use the Internet?

B Listen to the rest of the program. Then answer these questions.

What does the term "net evaders" mean?
What are "Internet dropouts"?
Why do some people become Internet dropouts?

7 CONVERSATION *I give up!*

A ▶ Listen and practice.

Terry: I give up! I can't figure this out.

Rachel: What's wrong?

Terry: I'm trying to create a song playlist for my party on Saturday.

Rachel: I can help. It's really easy. First, choose "New Playlist" from the menu.

Terry: Here? Oh, I see.

Rachel: Now type in the name of your playlist. Then go to your song file and choose the ones you want.

Terry: But how do I choose the songs?

Rachel: Just drag them to the playlist. Be sure to press these keys to highlight more than one song.

Terry: That *was* easy. Thanks! So are you coming on Saturday?

Rachel: Of course. But don't forget to include my favorite songs on your playlist, OK?

B ▶ Listen to the rest of the conversation. What else does Terry want help with?

8 GRAMMAR FOCUS

> ### Imperatives and infinitives for giving suggestions ▶
>
> **Be sure to** press these keys. **Don't forget to** include my favorite songs.
> **Make sure to** save your work. **Try not to** be late for the party.
> **Remember to** back up your files.

A Look at these suggestions. Which ones refer to (a) an alarm system? (b) a smartphone? (c) a laptop? (More than one answer is sometimes possible.)

1. Try to keep it closed to protect the screen. ....
2. Don't forget to write down your secret code. ....
3. Remember to turn it off as soon as you come in the door. ....
4. Try not to get it wet or the keys may get stuck. ....
5. Make sure to set it each time you leave home. ....
6. Remember to recharge the battery before it dies. ....
7. Be sure to turn it off before bed or a call may wake you up. ....
8. Make sure to keep the software up to date. ....

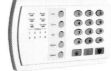

a

b

B **GROUP WORK** Take turns giving other suggestions for using the items in part A. Use these phrases.

Make sure to . . .	Try to . . .	Remember to . . .
Be sure not to . . .	Try not to . . .	Don't forget to . . .

c

9 LISTENING *Good suggestions*

A ▶ Listen to people give suggestions about three of these things. Number them 1, 2, and 3. (There are two extra things.)

MP4 player

ATM card

GPS system

video camera

flash drive

B ▶ Listen again. Write two suggestions you hear for each thing. Then compare with a partner.

1. ....
2. ....
3. ....

C PAIR WORK What do you know about the two other things in part A? What suggestions can you give about them?

10 INTERCHANGE 7 *Talk radio*

Give callers to a radio program some advice. Go to Interchange 7 on page 121.

11 WRITING *An email*

A Imagine you're sick today and can't go to class. A classmate has agreed to help you. Think of three things you need him or her to do for you. Then write an email with instructions.

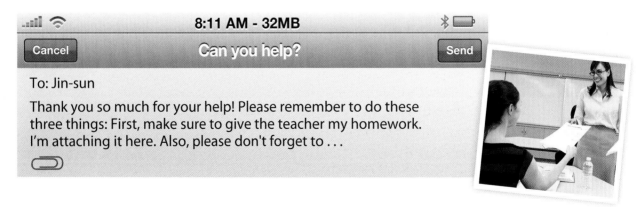

📶 📶 🔋   **8:11 AM - 32MB**   ✳ 🔋

| Cancel | Can you help? | Send |

To: Jin-sun

Thank you so much for your help! Please remember to do these three things: First, make sure to give the teacher my homework. I'm attaching it here. Also, please don't forget to . . .

B GROUP WORK Take turns reading your emails aloud. Do you have similar favors?

Modern-Day Treasure Hunters

Scan the article. What is geocaching? Who enjoys it? Why?

Geocaching is a game played worldwide – even though it only began in 2000! *Geo* is from the word *geography,* and *caching* (pronounced "cashing") means hiding a container with "treasure" inside. The purpose of geocaching is to use GPS technology to find a hidden cache – some people call it a high-tech treasure-hunting game. Technophiles love it because you need technology. Hikers love it because you may have to walk a long way. And looking for treasure is fun, so it's also great for children.

It isn't difficult to become a geocacher. First, buy a small handheld GPS device. Next, search online for a geocaching website and choose a cache to look for. Some caches are in beautiful locations, such as river valleys, mountains, or beaches. For each cache, websites list coordinates – numbers that give an exact geographical position (for example, 48°51.29' N, 02°17.40' E is the Eiffel Tower in Paris). Input the coordinates for your cache into your GPS device, and you're ready to go!

Your GPS device will identify the exact location of your cache. That's the easy part. The hard part comes after you get to the location – finding the cache! Some caches are hidden under stones, in trees, or even in water. And what will you find in your cache? If you're looking for gold or diamonds, you'll be very disappointed. Most caches contain inexpensive things like books, toys, coins, or DVDs. There's also a logbook and pencil for you to record the date you found the cache and make comments. The real prize is the pleasure of saying, "I found it!"

Geocaching etiquette allows you to take whatever you want from the cache, but you must replace it with something of the same or higher value. Don't forget to bring some treasure for the next geocacher!

A Read the article. Check (✓) True or False for each statement. Then correct each false statement.

True	False		
☐	✔	1. Geocaching is a new low-tech game.	It's a high-tech game.
☐	☐	2. Geocaching is popular in many countries.	
☐	☐	3. You need information from websites.	
☐	☐	4. Your GPS device gives you coordinates.	
☐	☐	5. Your GPS device finds cache locations for you.	
☐	☐	6. Caches contain pencils as well as treasure.	
☐	☐	7. Geocachers usually find gold.	
☐	☐	8. Geocaching is about giving and taking.	

B **PAIR WORK** Have you ever been geocaching? If so, did you enjoy it? If not, would you like to try it? Why or why not?

8 Let's celebrate!

1 ## SNAPSHOT

HOLIDAYS AND FESTIVALS

Chinese New Year
January or February
Chinese people celebrate the lunar new year with fireworks and lion dances.

Australia Day
January 26
Australians put on patriotic shows to celebrate their national day.

Children's Day
May 5
Japanese families put up colored streamers shaped like fish, in honor of their children.

Day of the Dead
November 2
Mexicans make playful skeleton sculptures and bake *pan de muerto* – bread of the dead.

Sources: *Reader's Digest Book of Facts*

Do you celebrate these or similar holidays in your country?
What other special days do you have?
What's your favorite holiday or festival?

WORD POWER Collocations

A Which word or phrase is not usually paired with each verb?
Put a line through it. Then compare with a partner.

1. **eat**	candy	rice cakes	~~juice~~
2. **give**	presents	relatives	candy
3. **go to**	decorations	a wedding	a party
4. **have**	a party	a beach	a meal
5. **play**	games	money	music
6. **send**	cards	flowers	a party
7. **visit**	relatives	food	friends
8. **watch**	a birthday	a parade	fireworks
9. **wear**	new clothes	a celebration	traditional clothes

B **PAIR WORK** Do you do any of the things in part A as part of a cultural or family celebration? When? Tell your partner.

3 PERSPECTIVES *Special days*

A ▶ Listen to these comments about special days of the year. Match them to the correct pictures.

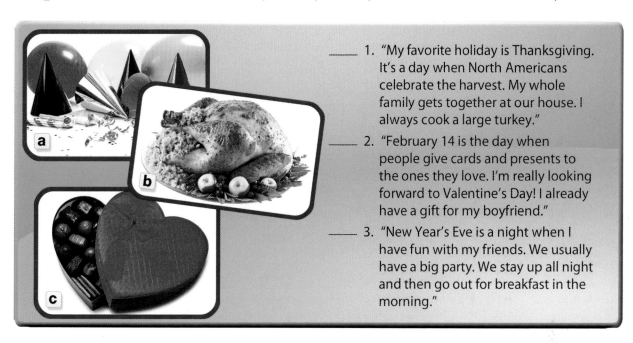

_____ 1. "My favorite holiday is Thanksgiving. It's a day when North Americans celebrate the harvest. My whole family gets together at our house. I always cook a large turkey."

_____ 2. "February 14 is the day when people give cards and presents to the ones they love. I'm really looking forward to Valentine's Day! I already have a gift for my boyfriend."

_____ 3. "New Year's Eve is a night when I have fun with my friends. We usually have a big party. We stay up all night and then go out for breakfast in the morning."

B PAIR WORK What do you like about each holiday in part A?

4 GRAMMAR FOCUS

> ### Relative clauses of time ▶
>
> | | |
> |---|---|
> | Thanksgiving is **a day** | **when** we celebrate the harvest. |
> | February 14 is **the day** | **when** people give cards to the ones they love. |
> | New Year's Eve is **a night** | **when** I have fun with my friends. |

A How much do you know about these times? Complete the sentences in column A with information from column B. Then compare with a partner.

A

1. New Year's Eve is a night when ....
2. April Fools' Day is a day when ....
3. Summer is a time when ....
4. Valentine's Day is a day when ....
5. Labor Day is a day when ....
6. Autumn is the season when ....

B

a. North Americans celebrate Thanksgiving.
b. students have a break from school.
c. people have parties with family and friends.
d. people in many countries honor workers.
e. people express their love to someone.
f. people sometimes play tricks on friends.

B Complete these sentences with your own information. Then compare with a partner.

Winter is the season . . .   Mother's Day is a day . . .
Birthdays are days . . .   July and August are the months . . .
Spring is the time of year . . .   A wedding anniversary is a time . . .

5 LISTENING Carnaval time

Carnaval in Brazil

A ⊙ Mike has just returned from Brazil. Listen to him talk about Carnaval. What was his favorite thing about it?

B ⊙ Listen again and answer these questions.

What is Carnaval?
How long does it last?
When is it?
What is the samba?

6 SPEAKING Favorite holidays

A **PAIR WORK** Choose your three favorite holidays. Tell your partner why you like each one.

A: I really like Republic Day.
B: What do you like about it?
A: Well, it's a time when schools and offices are closed, and we have parades and fireworks.

B **CLASS ACTIVITY** Take a class vote. What are the most popular holidays in your class?

Republic Day in Turkey

Mid-Autumn Festival in Singapore

7 WRITING An online entry

A Write an entry for a travel website about a festival or celebration where you live. When is it? How do people celebrate it? What should a visitor see and do?

> The annual fireworks festival in Yenshui, Taiwan, occurs on the last day of the New Year celebration. This is the first full moon of the new lunar year. It's a day when people explode fireworks in the streets, paint their faces, and dress up as . . .

B **PAIR WORK** Read your partner's entry. What do you like about it? Can you suggest anything to improve it?

8 CONVERSATION Wedding day

A ▶ Listen and practice.

Jill: Your wedding pictures are really beautiful, Emiko.

Emiko: Thank you. Those pictures are from right after the ceremony.

Jill: Where was the ceremony?

Emiko: At a shrine. When people get married in Japan, they sometimes have the ceremony at a shrine.

Jill: That's interesting. Were there a lot of people there?

Emiko: Well, usually only family members and close friends go to the ceremony. But afterward, we had a reception with family and friends.

Jill: So, what are receptions like in Japan?

Emiko: There's a big dinner, and after the meal, the guests give speeches or sing songs.

Jill: It sounds like fun.

Emiko: It really is. And then, before the guests leave, the bride and groom give them presents.

Jill: The guests get presents?

Emiko: Yes, and the guests give money to the bride and groom.

B ▶ Listen to the rest of the conversation. What did the bride and groom give each guest?

9 PRONUNCIATION Stress and rhythm

A ▶ Listen and practice. Notice how stressed words and syllables occur with a regular rhythm.

When people get married in Japan, they sometimes have the ceremony at a shrine.

B ▶ Listen to the stress and rhythm in these sentences. Then practice them.

1. After the ceremony, there's a reception with family and friends.

2. Before the guests leave, the bride and groom give them presents.

3. The guests usually give money to the bride and groom.

10 GRAMMAR FOCUS

Adverbial clauses of time ▸

When people get married in Japan,	they sometimes have the ceremony at a shrine.
After the food is served,	the guests give speeches or sing songs.
Before the guests leave,	the bride and groom give them presents.

A What do you know about wedding customs in North America?
Complete these sentences with the information below.

1. Before a man and woman get married, they usually ....
2. When a couple gets engaged, the man often ....
3. Right after a couple gets engaged, they usually ....
4. When a woman gets married, her family usually ....
5. When guests go to a wedding, they almost always ....
6. Right after a couple gets married, they usually ....

a. pays for the wedding and reception.
b. go on a short trip called a "honeymoon."
c. give the bride and groom a gift or some money.
d. gives the woman an engagement ring.
e. begin to plan the wedding.
f. date each other for a year or more.

B PAIR WORK What happens when people get married in your country?
Tell your partner by completing the statements in part A with your own
information. Pay attention to stress and rhythm.

11 INTERCHANGE 8 *Special occasions*

How do your classmates celebrate special occasions? Go to Interchange 8 on page 122.

12 SPEAKING *That's an interesting custom.*

A GROUP WORK Do you know any interesting customs related to the
topics below? Explain a custom and discuss it with your classmates.

births   courtship   good luck   marriages   seasons

A: I know a custom from the Philippines. When a
boy courts a girl, he stands outside her house
and sings to her.
B: What does he sing?
C: Romantic songs, of course!

B CLASS ACTIVITY Tell the class the most interesting
custom you talked about in your group.

Customs Around the World

1 On the third Monday of October, Jamaicans celebrate National Heroes' Day. They honor seven men and women who were important to Jamaica's history. There are speeches, music, sports, and dancing. They also give awards to "local heroes" for helping their communities.

2 On August 15 of the lunar calendar, Koreans celebrate Chusok, also known as Korean Thanksgiving. It's a day when people give thanks for the harvest. Korean families honor their ancestors by going to their graves to take them rice and fruit and clean the gravesites.

3 An interesting custom in Thailand is Loy Krathong. A krathong is a bowl made from the bark and leaves of banana trees. It's decorated with a lit candle, three lit joss sticks, and flowers. After the rainy season, on the evening of the full moon in November, Thai people float krathongs on the river to pay respect to the river goddess.

4 Finland has a unique but very modern custom. It started because some people felt angry when their cell phones didn't work well. They wanted to express their frustration in a humorous way. So every summer, there is a cell-phone-throwing contest. People throw their cell phones as far as possible. The winner receives a prize, such as a gold medal.

A Read the article. Then answer these questions.

1. When is National Heroes' Day in Jamaica?
2. Why do Koreans celebrate Chusok?
3. What do Thais do for Loy Krathong?
4. Why do Finns go to the cell-phone-throwing contest?

B What do these words refer to? Write the correct word(s).

1. They (par. 1, line 2) ....
2. their (par. 1, line 6) ....
3. It (par. 2, line 3) ....
4. It (par. 3, line 3) ....
5. It (par. 4, line 2) ....
6. They (par. 4, line 4) ....

C **PAIR WORK** Do you have a similar holiday or custom in your country? Describe it.

Units 7–8 Progress check

SELF-ASSESSMENT

How well can you do these things? Check (✓) the boxes.

I can	Very well	OK	A little
Describe uses and purposes of everyday objects (Ex. 1)	☐	☐	☐
Give instructions and advice (Ex. 2)	☐	☐	☐
Describe special days and customs (Ex. 3, 5)	☐	☐	☐
Understand descriptions of customs (Ex. 4, 5)	☐	☐	☐
Ask and answer questions about special days and customs (Ex. 5)	☐	☐	☐

1 GAME What is it?

A PAIR WORK Think of five familiar objects. Write a short description of each object's use and purpose. Don't write the name of the objects.

> It's electronic. You hold it in your hand. You look through it.
> You use it to make movies. It can sometimes be heavy.

B GROUP WORK Take turns reading your descriptions and guessing the objects. Keep score. Who guessed the most items correctly? Who wrote the best descriptions?

2 ROLE PLAY Stressful situations

Student A: Choose one situation below. Decide on the details and answer Student B's questions. Then get some suggestions.
Start like this: *I'm really nervous. I'm . . .*

going on a job interview	**taking my driving test**	**giving a speech**
What's the job?	When is it?	What is it about?
What are the responsibilities?	How long is it?	Where is it?
Who is interviewing you?	Have you prepared?	How many people will be there?

Student B: Student A is telling you about a situation.
Ask the appropriate questions above.
Then give some suggestions.

Change roles and try the role play again.

useful expressions	
Try to . . .	Try not to . . .
Remember to . . .	Be sure to . . .
Don't forget to . . .	Make sure to . . .

3 SPEAKING *My own holiday*

A **PAIR WORK** Choose one of these imaginary holidays or create your own.
Then write a description of the holiday. Answer the questions below.

World Smile Day

All-You-Can-Eat Cake Day

Be Late for Something Day

What is the name of the holiday? When is it? How do you celebrate it?

> World Smile Day is a day when you have to smile at everyone. It's on June 15, the last day of school. People have parties, and sometimes there's a parade!

B **GROUP WORK** Read your description to the group. Then vote on the best holiday.

4 LISTENING *Marriage customs*

A ⏵ Listen to some information about marriage customs. Check (✓) True or False.

True	False	
☐	☐	**1.** When two women of a tribe in Paraguay want to marry the same man, they have a boxing match. ....
☐	☐	**2.** When people get married in Malaysia, they have to eat cooked rice. ....
☐	☐	**3.** In Italy, before a couple gets married, a friend or relative releases two white doves. ....
☐	☐	**4.** In some parts of India, when people get married, water is poured over them. ....

B ⏵ Listen again. Correct the false statements.

5 DISCUSSION *In my country, . . .*

GROUP WORK Talk about marriage in your country. Ask these questions and others of your own.

How old are people when they get married?
What happens after a couple gets engaged?
What happens during the ceremony?
What do the bride and groom wear?
What kind of food is served at the reception?
What kinds of gifts do people usually give?

a Korean wedding tradition

WHAT'S NEXT?

Look at your Self-assessment again. Do you need to review anything?

Interchange activities

A **CLASS ACTIVITY** Go around the class and find out the information below. Then ask follow-up questions and take notes. Write a classmate's name only once.

Find someone who	Name	Notes
1. used to look very different **"Did you use to look very different?"**		
2. always listened to his or her teachers **"Did you always listen to your teachers?"**		
3. had a pet when he or she was little **"Did you have a pet when you were little?"**		
4. wanted to be a movie star **"Did you ever want to be a movie star?"**		
5. changed schools when he or she was a child "..?"		
6. used to argue with his or her brothers and sisters "..?"		
7. got in trouble a lot as a child "..?"		
8. used to have a favorite toy "..?"		

B **GROUP WORK** Tell the group the most interesting thing you learned about your classmates.

TOURISM CAMPAIGN

A **PAIR WORK** Look at the photos and slogans below. What do you think the theme of each tourism campaign is?

possible themes		
art	food	nature
culture	history	shopping
entertainment	music	sports

Rio de Janeiro
"Carnaval and Natural Marvels"

Cairo
"The Earth's Mother"

Hong Kong
"A Diner's Paradise"

Salzburg
"A Musical Banquet"

B **GROUP WORK** Imagine you are planning a campaign to attract more tourists to one of the cities above or to a city of your choice. Use the ideas below or your own ideas to discuss the campaign.

a good time to visit
famous historical attractions
special events or festivals
nice areas to stay
interesting places to see
memorable things to do

A: Do you know when a good time to visit Rio is?
B: I think February or March is a good time because . . .

C **GROUP WORK** What will be the theme of your campaign? What slogan will you use?

A Complete this questionnaire with information about yourself.

☆My Wish List

1. What kind of vacation do you wish you could take?
   I wish I could

2. What sport do you wish you could play?

3. Which country do you wish you could live in?

4. What kind of home do you wish you could have?

5. What kind of pet do you wish you could have?

6. What languages do you wish you could speak?

7. Which musical instruments do you wish you could play?

8. What kind of car do you wish you could buy?

9. What famous people do you wish you could meet?

10. What do you wish you could do right now?

B **PAIR WORK** Compare your questionnaires. Take turns asking and answering questions about your wishes.

A: What kind of vacation do you wish you could take?
B: I wish I could go on a safari.
A: Really? Why?
B: Well, I could take some great pictures of wild animals!

C **CLASS ACTIVITY** Imagine you are at a class reunion. It is ten years since you completed the questionnaire in part A. Tell the class about some wishes that have come true for your partner.

"Sue is a photographer now. She travels to Africa every year and takes pictures of wild animals. Her photos are in many magazines."

A How much do you really know about your classmates? Look at the survey and add two more situations to items 1 and 2.

	Name	Notes
1. Find someone who has . . .		
a. forgotten a password		
b. lost his or her phone		
c. been on TV		
d. cried during a movie		
e. sung in public		
f.		
g.		
2. Find someone who has never . . .		
a. driven a car		
b. used a recipe to cook		
c. played a video game		
d. baked cookies		
e. been camping		
f.		
g.		

B CLASS ACTIVITY Go around the class and ask the questions. Write the names of classmates who answer "yes" for item 1 and "no" for item 2. Then ask follow-up questions and take notes.

A: Have you ever forgotten a password?
B: Yes, I have.
A: Did you ever remember it?
B: Yes, but it took an hour!

A: Have you ever driven a car?
C: No, I haven't.
A: Why not?
C: Because I don't have a driver's license.

C GROUP WORK Compare the information in your surveys.

Student A

A PAIR WORK You and your partner are going to take a trip. You have a brochure for a biking trip, and your partner has a brochure for a surfing trip.

First, find out about the surfing trip. Ask your partner questions about these things.

the length of the trip	the cost of the trip	what the price includes
the accommodations	entertainment options	nighttime activities

B PAIR WORK Now use the information in this brochure to answer your partner's questions about the biking trip.

Colorado Biking Trip
14-day biking, camping, and hiking tour

Visit these beautiful sites in the Rocky Mountains:
- Estes Park
- The Continental Divide
- Peaceful Valley Lodge
- Gem Lake

Accommodations:
Deluxe campsites with hot showers

Price includes:
All meals, daily bicycle and equipment rental, bike safety class

Nighttime activities:
Campfire sing-alongs, stargazing, stories from the Old West

Additional activities:
- Hike in Rocky Mountain National Park
- Spot wildlife, such as elk, moose, and eagles
- Visit an old ghost town

Tour cost:
$1,699

C PAIR WORK Decide which trip you are going to take. Then explain your choice to the class.

THAT'S NO EXCUSE!

A PAIR WORK Look at these situations and act out conversations. Apologize and then give an excuse, admit a mistake, or make an offer or a promise.

useful expressions
I'm sorry. / I didn't realize. / I forgot.
You're right. / I was wrong.
I'll . . . right away.
I'll make sure to . . . / I promise I'll . . .

1

Student A: You're the customer.

Student B: You're the hairstylist.

A: My hair! You ruined my hair!
B: ....

2

Student A: You own the backpack.

Student B: You own the puppy.

A: Hey! Your puppy has my bag!
B: ....

3

Student A: You're driving the red car.

Student B: You're driving the blue car.

A: Watch where you're going!
B: ....

4

Student A: You're the customer.

Student B: You're the cashier.

A: Oh, dear. I don't seem to have any cash. . . .
B: ....

B GROUP WORK Have you ever experienced situations like these? What happened? What did you do? Share your stories.

Student B

A PAIR WORK You and your partner are going to take a trip. You have a brochure for a surfing trip, and your partner has a brochure for a biking trip.

First, use the information in this brochure to answer your partner's questions about the surfing trip.

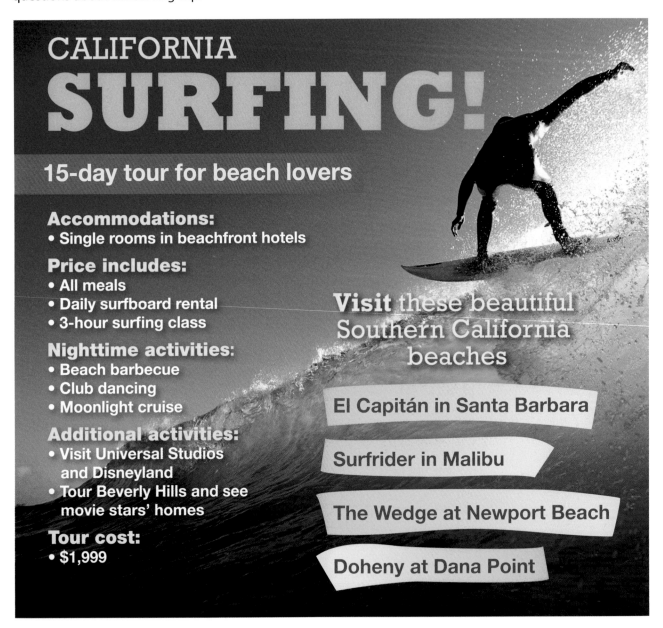

CALIFORNIA SURFING!

15-day tour for beach lovers

Accommodations:
• Single rooms in beachfront hotels

Price includes:
• All meals
• Daily surfboard rental
• 3-hour surfing class

Nighttime activities:
• Beach barbecue
• Club dancing
• Moonlight cruise

Additional activities:
• Visit Universal Studios and Disneyland
• Tour Beverly Hills and see movie stars' homes

Tour cost:
• $1,999

Visit these beautiful Southern California beaches

El Capitán in Santa Barbara

Surfrider in Malibu

The Wedge at Newport Beach

Doheny at Dana Point

B PAIR WORK Now find out about the biking trip. Ask your partner questions about these things.

the length of the trip   the cost of the trip   what the price includes
the accommodations   entertainment options   nighttime activities

C PAIR WORK Decide which trip you are going to take. Then explain your choice to the class.

A GROUP WORK Look at the four problems that people called a radio program about. What advice would you give each caller? Discuss possible suggestions and then choose the best one.

Caller 1: My family and I are going away on vacation. How can we make sure our home is safe from burglars while we're gone?

Caller 2: A classmate wants to borrow my MP3 player to take with him on vacation. I don't want to lend it to him. What can I say?

Caller 3: I'm going to meet my girlfriend's parents tomorrow for the first time. How can I make a good impression?

Caller 4: I'm really into social networking, but in the past week, five people I hardly know have asked me to be their friend.

You have 5 new friend requests

B PAIR WORK Take turns "calling" a radio station and explaining your problems. Use the situations above or create new ones. Your partner should give you advice.

A: My family and I are going away on vacation. How can we make sure our home is safe from burglars while we're gone?
B: Well, don't forget to lock all the windows. Oh, and make sure to . . .

SPECIAL OCCASIONS

A **CLASS ACTIVITY** How do your classmates celebrate special
occasions? Go around the class and ask the questions below. If someone
answers "yes," write down his or her name. Ask for more information
and take notes.

QUESTION	NAME	NOTES
1. Does your family have big get-togethers?		
2. Have you bought flowers for someone special recently?		
3. Do you like to watch street parades?		
4. Do you ever wear traditional clothes?		
5. Has someone given you money recently as a gift?		
6. Have you ever given someone a surprise birthday party?		
7. Will you celebrate your next birthday with a party?		
8. Did you get any cards on your last birthday?		
9. Do you ever give friends birthday presents?		
10. Is New Year's your favorite time of the year?		
11. Do you ever celebrate a holiday with fireworks?		

A: Does your family have big get-togethers?
B: Yes, we do.
A: What do you do when you get together?
B: Well, we have a big meal. After we eat, we play games and watch old home movies.

B **PAIR WORK** Compare your information with a partner.

Notes

Grammar plus

Unit 1

1 Past tense (page 3)

▶ Use a form of *be* with *born*: I **was born** here. (NOT: I ~~born~~ here.) Don't use a form of *be* with the verb *die*: He **died** last year. (NOT: He ~~was died~~ last year.)

Complete the conversation.

1. A: Do you live around here?
   B: No, I don't. I'm from Costa Rica.
   A: Really? _Were you born_ in Costa Rica?
   B: No. Actually, I was born in Santiago, Panama.
2. A: That's interesting. So where .... ?
   B: I grew up in Costa Rica. My family moved there when I was little.
3. A: .... in the capital?
   B: No, my family didn't live in a city. We lived in a small town called Grecia.
4. A: .... away from Grecia?
   B: Oh, about eight years ago. I left Grecia to go to college.
5. A: Where .... to college?
   B: I went to college in San Jose, and I live there now.
6. A: And .... to Miami?
   B: I got here a few days ago. I'm visiting my cousin.

2 *Used to* (page 5)

▶ Use the base form of *used to* in questions and negative statements: Did you **use to** play sports? (NOT: Did you ~~used to~~ play sports?) I didn't **use to** like bananas. (NOT: I didn't ~~used to~~ like bananas.)
▶ Don't use *never* in negative statements: I **never used to** wear sunglasses. (NOT: I never ~~didn't use to~~ wear sunglasses.)

Complete the conversations with the correct form of *used to*.

1. A: Hey, Dad. What kinds of clothes _did you use to_ wear – you know, when you were a kid?
   B: Oh, we .... wear jeans and T-shirts – like you kids do now.
   A: Really? .... Mom .... dress like that, too?
   B: No, not really. She never .... like wearing pants. She always .... wear skirts and dresses.
2. A: .... you .... play a sport when you were a kid?
   B: Well, I .... be a swimmer. My sister and I .... swim on a team.
   A: Wow, that's cool! Were you good?
   B: Yeah. I .... win gold medals all the time. And my sister .... be the fastest swimmer on the team.

Unit 2

1 Expressions of quantity (page 9)

▶ Count nouns have a plural form that usually ends in -s. Noncount nouns don't have a plural form because you can't separate and count them: Are there any **parking garages** around here? BUT Is there any **parking** around here? (NOT: Are there any ~~parkings~~ around here?)

Complete the conversations with the correct words in parentheses.

1. A: There's .... (too many / too much) traffic in this city. There should be .... (fewer / less) cars downtown.
   B: The problem is there .... (aren't / isn't) enough public transportation.
   A: You're right. We should have more .... (bus / buses). There .... (aren't / isn't) enough of them during rush hour.
2. A: How do you like your new neighborhood?
   B: It's terrible, actually. There's .... (too many / too much) noise and .... (too few / too little) parking.
   A: That's too bad. There .... (aren't / isn't) enough parking spaces in my neighborhood either.
3. A: Did you hear about the changes to the city center? Starting next month, there will be more bicycle .... (lane / lanes) and .... (fewer / less) street parking.
   B: That's good. There .... (are too many / is too much) pollution downtown. I'm sure there will be .... (fewer / less) accidents, too.
   A: That's true.

2 Indirect questions from Wh-questions (page 11)

▶ Indirect questions are often polite requests for information. *Can you tell me how much this magazine costs?* sounds more polite than *How much does this magazine cost?*

Complete the conversation with indirect questions.

1. A: Excuse me. Can you *tell me where the post office is* .... ?
   B: Yes, of course. The post office is on the next corner.
2. A: And could you .... ?
   B: You can find a really good restaurant on Central Avenue.
3. A: OK. Do you .... ?
   B: Yes. The restaurant is called Giorgio's.
4. A: Thanks. Can you .... ?
   B: Yes. They serve Italian food.
5. A: Oh, good! Do you .... ?
   B: It opens at 5:00. Tell them Joe sent you!
   A: OK, Joe. Thanks for everything! Bye now.

Unit 3

1 Evaluations and comparisons (page 17)

▶ In evaluations, *enough* goes after adjectives and before nouns.
adjective + *enough*: This house isn't **bright enough**. (NOT: This house isn't ~~enough bright~~.
noun + *enough*: This house doesn't have **enough light**. (NOT: This house doesn't have ~~light enough~~.)

A Read each situation. Then write two sentences describing the problem, one sentence with *not . . . enough* and one with *too*.

1. Our family needs a big house. This house is very small.
   a. *This house isn't big enough for us.*
   b. *This house is too small for us.*
2. We want to live on a quiet street. This street is very noisy.
   a. ....
   b. ....
3. We need three bedrooms. This house has only two.
   a. ....
   b. ....
4. We want a spacious living room. This one is cramped.
   a. ....
   b. ....

B Rewrite the comparisons using *as . . . as*. Use *just* when possible.

1. My new apartment is smaller than my old one.
   My new apartment isn't as large as my old one.
2. This neighborhood is safer than my old one.
   ....
3. This apartment has a lot of privacy. My old one did, too.
   ....
4. My rent is reasonable now. It was very high before.
   ....

2 *Wish* (page 20)

▶ Use *could* (the past of *can*) and *would* (the past of *will*) with *wish*: I **can't** move right now, but I wish I **could**. My landlord **won't** paint my apartment, but I wish he **would**.

Match the problems with the wishes.

1. My house isn't very nice. ...c...
2. It costs a lot to live here. ....
3. My landlord won't call me back. ....
4. I have noisy neighbors. ....
5. I don't like living alone. ....
6. The buses don't run very often. ....

a. I wish I could find a good roommate.
b. I wish he'd return my calls.
c. I wish it were more attractive.
d. I wish I could afford a car.
e. I wish their music weren't so loud.
f. I wish it weren't so expensive.

Unit 4

1 Simple past vs. present perfect (page 23)

▶ Use the simple past – not the present perfect – when you say when an event ended: I **had** sushi <u>last night</u>. (NOT: I've had sushi last night.)

Complete the conversations. Choose the best forms.

1. A: What .... (did you have / have you had) for dinner last night?
    B: I .... (tried / have tried) Indian food for the first time. .... (Did you ever have / Have you ever had) it?
    A: A friend and I .... (ate / have eaten) at an Indian restaurant just last week. It .... (was / has been) delicious!
2. A: .... (Did you ever take / Have you ever taken) a cooking class?
    B: No, I .... (didn't / haven't). How about you?
    A: I .... (took / have taken) a few classes. My last class .... (was / has been) in December. We .... (learned / have learned) how to make some wonderful Spanish dishes.
3. A: I .... (watched / have watched) a great cooking show on TV yesterday.
    B: Really? I .... (never saw / have never seen) a cooking show. .... (Was it / Has it been) boring?
    A: No, it .... (wasn't / hasn't). It .... (was / has been) very interesting!

2 Sequence adverbs (page 25)

▶ *Then, next,* and *after that* mean the same. *First* comes first, and *finally* comes last; you can use the other adverbs in any order: **First,** put some water in a pan. **Then/Next,/ After that,** put the eggs in the water. **Finally,** boil the eggs for seven minutes.

Unscramble the steps in this recipe for hamburgers. Then write the steps in order.

salt and pepper   add   in the bowl   to the meat   then

.... : ....

two pounds of chopped beef   put   in a bowl   first,

...Step 1... : First, put two pounds of chopped beef in a bowl.

put   the burgers   in a pan   finally,   and cook for 10 minutes

.... : ....

next,   the meat   and the salt and pepper   mix   together

.... : ....

into four burgers   after that,   with your hands   form the meat

.... : ....

Unit 5

1 Future with *be going to* and *will* (page 31)

▶ Use the base form of the verb – not the infinitive (*to* + base form) – with *will*: I think **I'll go** to Hawaii next winter. (NOT: I think I'll ~~to~~ go to Hawaii next winter.)

▶ Use *be going to* – not *will* – when you know something is going to happen: Look at those black clouds. It**'s going to** rain. (NOT: It ~~will~~ rain.)

Complete the conversation with the correct form of *be going to* or *will* and the verbs in parentheses.

A: It's Friday – at last! What ..are.you.going.to.do.. (do) this weekend?

B: I'm not sure. I'm really tired, so I probably .... (not do) anything exciting. Maybe I .... (see) a movie on Saturday. How about you? How .... (spend) your weekend?

A: My wife and I .... (do) some work on our house. We .... (paint) the living room on Saturday. On Sunday, we .... (clean) all the rugs.

B: .... (do) anything fun?

A: Oh, I think we .... (have) a lot of fun. We like working around the house. And Sunday's my birthday, so we .... (have) dinner at my favorite Italian restaurant.

B: Now that sounds like fun!

2 Modals for necessity and suggestion (page 33)

▶ Some modals for necessity and suggestion are stronger than others.
Weak (for advice or an opinion): *should, ought to*
Stronger (for a warning): *had better*
Strongest (for an obligation): *must, need to, have to*

Choose the correct word or words to complete the advice to travelers.

1. You .... (must / should) show identification at the airport. They won't allow you on a plane without an official ID.
2. Your ID .... (needs to / ought to) have a picture of you on it. It's required.
3. The picture of you .... (has to / ought to) be recent. They won't accept an old photo.
4. Travelers .... (must / should) get to the airport at least two hours before their flight. It's not a good idea to get there later than that.
5. All travelers .... (have to / had better) go through airport security. It's necessary for passenger safety.
6. Many airlines don't serve food, so passengers on long flights probably .... (must / ought to) buy something to eat at the airport.

Unit 6

1 Two-part verbs; *will* for responding to requests (page 37)

▶ Two-part verbs are verb + particle.
▶ If the object of a two-part verb is a noun, the noun can come before or after the particle: **Take out** the trash./**Take** the trash **out**.
▶ If the object is a pronoun, the pronoun must come before the particle: **Take** it **out**. (NOT: Take ~~out it~~.)

Write conversations. First, rewrite the request given by changing the position of the particle. Then write a response to the request using *it* or *them*.

1. Put away your clothes, please.
   A: Put your clothes away, please.
   B: OK. I'll put them away.
2. Turn the lights on, please.
   A: ....
   B: ....
3. Please turn your music down.
   A: ....
   B: ....
4. Clean up the kitchen, please.
   A: ....
   B: ....
5. Turn off your phone, please.
   A: ....
   B: ....

2 Requests with modals and *Would you mind ... ?* (page 39)

▶ Use the base form of the verb – not the infinitive (*to* + base form) – with the modals *can, could,* and *would*: **Could** you **get** me a sandwich? (NOT: Could you ~~to~~ get me a sandwich?)
▶ Requests with modals and *Would you mind ... ?* are polite – even without *please. Can you get me a sandwich?* sounds much more polite than *Get me a sandwich.*

Change these sentences to polite requests. Use the words in parentheses.

1. Bring in the mail. (could)
   Could you bring in the mail?
   ....
2. Put your shoes by the door. (would you mind)
   ....
3. Don't leave dishes in the sink. (would you mind)
   ....
4. Change the TV channel. (can)
   ....
5. Don't play ball inside. (would you mind)
   ....
6. Clean up your mess. (would you mind)
   ....
7. Put away the clean towels. (can)
   ....
8. Pick up your things. (could)
   ....

Unit 7

1 Infinitives and gerunds for uses and purposes (page 45)

▶ Sentences with infinitives and gerunds mean the same: *I use my cell phone to send text messages* means the same as *I use my cell phone for sending text messages.* Use a gerund – not an infinitive – after *for*: Satellites are used **for studying** weather. (NOT: Satellites are used for ~~to study~~ weather.)

Read each sentence about a technology item. Write two sentences about the item's use and purpose. Use the information in parentheses.

1. My sister's car has a built-in GPS system. (She use / get directions)
   a. *She uses the GPS system to get directions.*
   b. *She uses the GPS system for getting directions.*
2. I love my new smartphone. (I use / take pictures)
   a. ....
   b. ....
3. That's a flash drive. (You use / back up files)
   a. ....
   b. ....
4. My little brother wants his own laptop. (would only use / watch movies and play games)
   a. ....
   b. ....
5. I'm often on my computer all day long. (I use / shop online and do research)
   a. ....
   b. ....

2 Imperatives and infinitives for giving suggestions (page 47)

▶ With imperatives and infinitives, *not* goes before – not after – *to*: Try **not to** talk too long. (NOT: Try ~~to not~~ talk too long.)

Rewrite the sentences as suggestions. Use the words in parentheses.

1. When you go to the movies, turn off your phone. (don't forget)
   When you go to the movies, don't forget to turn off your phone.
2. Don't talk on the phone when you're in an elevator. (try)
   ....
3. Don't eat or drink anything when you're at the computer. (be sure)
   ....
4. Clean your computer screen and keyboard once a week. (remember)
   ....
5. Don't use your tablet outside when it's raining. (make sure)
   ....
6. When the bell rings to start class, put your music player away! (be sure)
   ....

Unit 8

1 Relative clauses of time (page 51)

▶ Relative clauses with *when* describe the word *time* or a noun that refers to a period of time, such as *day, night, month,* and *year.*

Combine the two sentences using *when.*

1. Thanksgiving is a holiday. Entire families get together.
   Thanksgiving is a holiday when entire families get together.
2. It's a wonderful time. People give thanks for the good things in their lives.

3. It's a day. Everyone eats much more than usual.

4. I remember one particular year. The whole family came to our house.

5. That year was very cold. It snowed all Thanksgiving day.

6. I remember another thing about that Thanksgiving. My brother and I baked eight pies.

2 Adverbial clauses of time (page 54)

▶ An adverbial clause of time can come before or after the main clause. When it comes before the main clause, use a comma. When it comes after the main clause, don't use a comma: When Ginny and Tom met, they both lived in San Juan. BUT: Ginny and Tom met when they both lived in San Juan.
▶ The words *couple* and *family* are collective nouns. They are usually used with singular verbs: When a couple **gets** married, they often receive gifts. (NOT: When a couple get married, they often receive gifts.)

Combine the two sentences using the adverb in parentheses. Write one sentence with the adverbial clause before the main clause and another with the adverbial clause after the main clause.

1. Students complete their courses. A school holds a graduation ceremony. (after)
   a. After students complete their courses, a school holds a graduation ceremony.
   b. A school holds a graduation ceremony after students complete their courses.
2. Students gather to put on robes and special hats. The ceremony starts. (before)
   a.
   b.
3. Music plays. The students walk in a line to their seats. (when)
   a.
   b.
4. School officials and teachers make speeches. Students get their diplomas. (after)
   a.
   b.
5. The ceremony is finished. Students throw their hats into the air and cheer. (when)
   a.
   b.

Grammar plus answer key

Unit 1

1 Past tense

2. did you grow up/are you from
3. Did you live
4. When did you move
5. did you go
6. when did you come/get

2 *Used to*

1. A: Hey, Dad. What kinds of clothes **did you use to** wear – you know, when you were a kid?
   B: Oh, we **used to** wear jeans and T-shirts – like you kids do now.
   A: Really? **Did** Mom **use to** dress like that, too?
   B: No, not really. She never **used to** like wearing pants. She always **used to** wear skirts and dresses.
2. A: **Did** you **use to** play a sport when you were a kid?
   B: Well, I **used to** be a swimmer. My sister and I **used to** swim on a team.
   A: Wow, that's cool! Were you good?
   B: Yeah. I **used to** win gold medals all the time. And my sister **used to** be the fastest swimmer on the team.

Unit 2

1 Expressions of quantity

1. A: There's **too much** traffic in this city. There should be **fewer** cars downtown.
   B: The problem is there **isn't** enough public transportation.
   A: You're right. We should have more **buses**. There **aren't** enough of them during rush hour.
2. A: How do you like your new neighborhood?
   B: It's terrible, actually. There's **too much** noise and **too little** parking.
   A: That's too bad. There **aren't** enough parking spaces in my neighborhood either.
3. A: Did you hear about the changes to the city center? Starting next month, there will be more bicycle **lanes** and **less** street parking.
   B: That's good. There **is too much** pollution downtown. I'm sure there will be **fewer** accidents, too.
   A: That's true.

2 Indirect questions from Wh-questions

Answers may vary. Some possible answers:

2. And could you **tell me where I can find a good restaurant**?
3. Do you **know what the name of the restaurant is**?
4. Can you **tell me what type of food they serve**?
5. Do you **know what time the restaurant opens**?

Unit 3

1 Evaluations and comparisons

A

Answers may vary. Some possible answers:

2. This street isn't quiet enough.
   This street is too noisy.
3. This house doesn't have enough bedrooms.
   This house is too small for us.
   This house has too few bedrooms for us.
4. This living room isn't spacious enough.
   This living room doesn't have enough space.
   This living room is too cramped/small.

B

Answers may vary. Some possible answers:

2. My old neighborhood isn't as safe as this one.
3. This apartment has (just) as much privacy as my old one.
4. My rent isn't as high as it used to be.

2 *Wish*

2. f   3. b   4. e   5. a   6. d

Unit 4

1 Simple past vs. present perfect

1. A: What **did you have** for dinner last night?
   B: I **tried** Indian food for the first time. **Have you ever had** it?
   A: A friend and I **ate** at an Indian restaurant just last week. It **was** delicious!
2. A: **Have you ever taken** a cooking class?
   B: No, **I haven't**. How about you?
   A: I **have taken** a few classes. My last class **was** in December. We **learned** how to make some wonderful Spanish dishes.
3. A: I **watched** a great cooking show on TV yesterday.
   B: Really? I **have never seen** a cooking show. **Was it** boring?
   A: No, it **wasn't**. It **was** very interesting!

2 Sequence adverbs

Step 1: First, put 2 pounds of chopped beef in a bowl.
Step 2: Then add salt and pepper to the meat in the bowl.
Step 3: Next, mix the meat and the salt and pepper together.
Step 4: After that, form the meat into four burgers with your hands.
Step 5: Finally, put the burgers in a pan and cook for ten minutes.

Unit 5

1 Future with *be going to* and *will*

B: I'm not sure. I'm really tired, so I probably **won't do** anything exciting. Maybe I'**ll see** a movie on Saturday. How about you? How **are you going to spend** your weekend?

A: My wife and I **are going to do** some work on our house. We'**re going to paint** the living room on Saturday. On Sunday, we'**re going to clean** all the rugs.

B: **Are(n't) you going to do** anything fun?

A: Oh, I think we'**ll have/'re going to have** a lot of fun. We like working around the house. And Sunday's my birthday, so we'**re going to have** dinner at my favorite Italian restaurant.

B: Now that sounds like fun!

2 Modals for necessity and suggestions

1. You **must** show identification at the airport. They won't allow you on a plane without an official ID.
2. Your ID **needs to** have a picture of you on it. It's required.
3. The picture of you **has to** be recent. They won't accept an old photo.
4. Travelers **should** get to the airport at least two hours before their flight. It's not a good idea to get there later than that.
5. All travelers **have to** go through airport security. It's necessary for passenger safety.
6. Many airlines don't serve food, so passengers on long flights probably **ought to** buy something to eat at the airport.

Unit 6

1 Two-part verbs; *will* for responding to requests

2. A: Turn on the lights, please.
   B: OK. I'll turn them on.
3. A: Please turn down your music.
   B: OK. I'll turn it down.
4. A: Clean the kitchen up, please.
   B: OK. I'll clean it up.
5. A: Turn your phone off, please.
   B: OK. I'll turn it off.

2 Requests with modals and *Would you mind . . . ?*

2. Would you mind putting your shoes by the door?
3. Would you mind not leaving dishes in the sink?
4. Can you change the TV channel?
5. Would you mind not playing ball inside?
6. Would you mind cleaning up your mess?
7. Can you put away the clean towels?
8. Could you pick up your things?

Unit 7

1 Infinitives and gerunds for uses and purposes

2. a. I use my smartphone/it to take pictures.
   b. I use my smartphone/it for taking pictures.
3. a. You use a flash drive/it to back up files.
   b. You use a flash drive/it for backing up files.
4. a. He would only use a laptop/it to watch movies and play games.
   b. He would only use a laptop/it for watching movies and playing games.
5. a. I use my computer/it to shop online and do research.
   b. I use my computer/it for shopping online and doing research.

2 Imperatives and infinitives for giving suggestions

2. Try not to talk on the phone when you're in an elevator.
3. Be sure not to eat or drink anything when you're at the computer.
4. Remember to clean your computer screen and keyboard once a week.
5. Make sure not to use your tablet outside when it's raining.
6. When the bell rings to start class, be sure to put your music player away!

Unit 8

1 Relative clauses of time

2. It's a wonderful time when people give thanks for the good things in their lives.
3. It's a day when everyone eats much more than usual.
4. I remember one particular year when the whole family came to our house.
5. That was a very cold year/Thanksgiving when it snowed all (Thanksgiving) day.
6. That was also the year/Thanksgiving when my brother and I baked eight pies.

2 Adverbial clauses of time

2. a. Students gather to put on robes and special hats before the ceremony starts.
   b. Before the ceremony starts, students gather to put on robes and special hats.
3. a. When the music plays, the students walk in a line to their seats.
   b. The students walk in a line to their seats when the music plays.
4. a. After school officials and teachers make speeches, students get their diplomas.
   b. Students get their diplomas after school officials and teachers make speeches.
5. a. When the ceremony is finished, students throw their hats into the air and cheer.
   b. Students throw their hats into the air and cheer when the ceremony is finished.

Credits

Illustrations

Andrezzinho: 16 (*top*), 43 (*top*), 62; **Ilias Arahovitis:** 37; **Mark Collins:** v, 16 (*bottom*), 36 (*top*), 41, 67 (*top*); **Carlos Diaz:** 39, 46, 93 (*bottom*), 104 (*center*), 114; **Jada Fitch:** 65, 119; **Travis Foster:** 20, 40 (*top*), 90 (*top*), 97 (*center*), 116 (*bottom*); **Chuck Gonzales:** 2, 30 (*bottom*), 64 (*bottom*), 106, 117; **Jim Haynes:** 36 (*bottom*), 75, 79, 99; **Trevor Keen:** 38, 61, 102, 121; **Jim Kelly:** 95 (*bottom earbuds, cell phone*) ; **Joanna Kerr:** 123; **KJA-artists:** 124 (*bottom*), 130; **Shelton Leong:** 22 (*bottom*), 58 (*bottom*), 108, 109; **Karen Minot:** 25 (*top*), 27, 32, 64 (*top*), 68, 72 (*top*), 76, 78, 90 (*bottom*), 105, 118, 129, 131; **Rob Schuster:** 8, 13, 18, 35, 40 (*bottom*), 44 (*early smartphone*), 50, 58 (*top*), 67 (*bottom*), 77, 86, 97, 122, 125; **Daniel Vasconcellos:** 15, 82, 110, 112; **Brad Walker:** 81, 100 (*bottom*); **Sam Whitehead:** 5, 6, 33, 43 (*bottom*), 53, 54, 92 (*bottom*), 93 (*top*), 127; **Jeff Wong:** 60; **James Yamasaki:** 19, 25 (*bottom*), 80, 94, 111; 128; **Rose Zgodzinski:** 2, 10, 22 (*top*), 30 (*top*), 44 (*top*), 55, 69, 78 (*top*), 92 (*top*), 120, 124 (*top*); **Carol Zuber-Mallison:** 7, 21, 26, 44 (*bottom*), 49, 63, 83, 85, 91, 100 (*top*), 104 (*bottom*), 116 (*top*), 126

Photos

2 (*left*) © Leslie Banks/iStockphoto; (*right*) © Jacqueline Veissid/Lifesize/ Getty Images
3 © MIXA/Getty Images
6 © Stretch Photography/Blend Images/age fotostock
7 (*clockwise from top*) © Steve Granitz/WireImage/Getty Images; © MGM Studios/Moviepix/Getty Images; © Photos 12/Alamy
8 (*top middle*) © Ilene MacDonald/Alamy; (*top right*) © Temmuz Can Arsiray/iStockphoto; (*bottom, clockwise from left*) © Jeff Morgan 09/ Alamy; © Peter Treanor/Alamy; © Daniel Borzynski/Alamy
9 © B. O'Kane/Alamy
11 © Zero Creatives/Cultura/Getty Images
13 (*top row*) © AP Photo/Uwe Lein; © AP Photo/Kydpl Kyodo; © Andrew Robinson/Alamy; © Courtesy of Wheelman Inc.
14 © Superstock/Getty Images
17 (*left to right*) © Imagemore Co. Ltd./Getty Images; © Niels Poulsen Mus/Alamy
18 © Yusuke Nakanishi/Aflo Foto Agency/Alamy
19 © Creatas/Punchstock
21 © Image100/age fotostock
22 (*top row*) © Topic Photo Agency/age fotostock; © Nico Tondini/age fotostock; © Eising/Bon Appetit/Alamy; © JTB Photo/SuperStock
23 © Juice Images/Alamy
24 (*top row*) © Jupiter Images/Foodpix/Getty Images; (*middle row*) © iStockphoto/Thinkstock; © Dave King/Dorling Kindersley/Getty Images; © Olga Utlyakova/iStockphoto; © funkyfood London-Paul Williams/Alamy; © John Kelly/Food Image Source/StockFood; © Eiichi Onodera/Getty Images
25 (*top left*) © Archive Photos/Stringer/Getty Images; (*middle row*) © George Kerrigan
26 (*top row*) © Shipes/Shooter/StockFood; © Olivier Blondeau/ iStockphoto; © Brent Melton/iStockphoto; © Boris Ryzhkov/iStockphoto; © Morten Olsen/iStockphoto; (*middle right*) © Asiaselects/Getty Images; (*bottom right*) © Debbi Smirnoff/iStockphoto
27 (*top right*) © Altrendo/Getty Images; (*middle right*) © Sean Justice/ Getty Images
29 (*middle right*) © Jiri Hera/Shutterstock; (*bottom right*) © AP Photo/ Shizuo Kambayashi
30 (*top row*) © Travelscape Images/Alamy; © Chicasso/Blend/Getty Images; © i love images/Veer; © Larry Williams/LWA/Blend Images/Alamy
31 © Julien Capmeil/Photonica/Getty Images
34 (*middle right*) © Irene Alastruey/age fotostock; (*bottom left*) © Teresa Kasprzycka/Shutterstock
35 © Jeff Greenberg/Alamy
38 © UpperCut Images/Getty Images
42 © Tyler Stableford/Stone/Getty Images
44 (*clockwise from left*) © Jowita Stachowiak/iStockphoto; © SSPL/ Getty Images; © RubberBall/Alamy; © David J. Green-studio/Alamy; © iStockphoto/Thinkstock; © Suto Norbert Zsolt/Shutterstock; © 7505811966/Shutterstock; © Oleksiy Mark/Shutterstock
45 (*top right*) © Mark Evans/iStockphoto; (*middle right*) © Schiller/ F1online digitale Bildagentur GmbH/Alamy
46 © Sullivan/Corbis
47 (*top row*) © Jupiterimages/Comstock Images/Getty Images; (*bottom right, top to bottom*) © Miles Boyer/Shutterstock; © Mark Evans/ iStockphoto; © broker/Veer
48 (*top row*) © mbbirdy/iStockphoto; © Maxim Pavlov/Veer; © Scanrail/ Fotolia; © gabyjalbert/iStockphoto; © Christophe Testi/Shutterstock; (*bottom right*) © Monashee Frantz/Ojo Images/age fotostock
49 (*right, top to bottom*) © Jurgen Wiesler/Imagebroker/Alamy; © Alfaguarilla/Shutterstock

50 (*top row*) © Roberto Gerometta/Lonely Planet Images/Getty Images; © David Hancock/Alamy; © Toru Yamanaka/AFP/Getty Images; © Tipograffias/Shutterstock
51 (*clockwise from top*) © Michael Flippo/Fotolia; © Olga Lyubkina/ iStockphoto; © DNY59/iStockphoto
52 (*top left*) © Masterfile; (*middle*) © AP Photo/Ibrahim Usta; (*middle right*) © Jack Hollingsworth/Asia Images//age fotostock; (*bottom right*) © Andy Chen/Flickr/Getty Images
53 © Christian Kober/AWL Images /Getty Images
55 (*top left*) © AP Photo/Collin Reid; (*top right*) © Michel Setboun/Corbis; (*middle left*) © Mickael David/Author's Image Ltd/Alamy; (*middle right*) © Ville Myllynen/AFP/Getty Images/NEWSCOM
56 © iStockphoto/Thinkstock
57 © Esbin Anderson/Photo Network/Alamy
58 (*top row*) © FPG/Retrofile/Getty Images; © Ariel Skelley/Blend Images/ Corbis; © Colin Anderson/Blend Images/Corbis
59 © Evening Standard/Stringer/Hulton Archive /Getty Images
60 © Engine Images/Fotolia
63 © Lane Oatey/Getty Images
67 (*bottom row*) © PBNJ Productions/Blend Images/Getty Images; © imagebroker.net/SuperStock; © Joe McBride/Stone/Getty Images
69 © Peter Dazeley/Photographer's Choice/Getty Images
71 (*middle row*) © Peter Dazeley/The Image Bank/Getty Images; © Topic Photo Agency/age fotostock; © Digital Vision/Photodisc/Thinkstock
72 (*top row*) © Dinodia/age fotostock; © Angelo Cavalli/age fotostock; © Jean-Paul Azam/The Image Bank/Getty Images; © Siegfried Layda/ Photographer's Choice/Getty Images; © Renault Philippe/Hemis/Alamy; (*bottom right*) © Mathias Beinling/Alamy
73 © Javier Soriano/AFP/Getty Images
74 (*middle row*) © iStockphoto/Thinkstock; © Takashi Katahira/Amana Images/Corbis; © Keren Su/Corbis
76 (*right, top to bottom*) © Mardagada/Alamy; © Timothy Fadek/Corbis; (*bottom right*) © Jim Holmes/Axiom Photographic Agency/Getty Images
77 (*top row*) © Yvette Cardozo/Alamy; © Robert Harding Picture Library/ SuperStock; © Oliver Berg/epa/Corbis
78 (*top row*) © Jeff Sarpa/StockFood Creative/Getty Images; © Stocksnapper/Alamy; © Pando Hall/Photographer's Choice/Getty Images; (*bottom left*) © Cultura Creative/Alamy
80 © AP Photo/Xie zhengyi/Imaginechina
83 (*top right*) © La Belle Kinoise/AFP/Getty Images/NEWSCOM; (*middle left*) © Urman Lionel/SIPA/NEWSCOM
84 © 20th Century Fox Film Corp./Everett Collection
86 (*left, top to bottom*) © AF archive/Alamy; © 20th Century Fox Film Corp./Everett Collection; (*right, top to bottom*) © AP Photo/Murray Close; © 20th Century Fox Film Corp./Everett Collection; (*bottom right*) © Mario Anzuoni/Reuters/Corbis
87 © Vera Anderson/WireImage/Getty Images
89 © Razorpix/Alamy
90 © David James/Twentieth Century Fox/Everett Collection
91 © Richard Foreman/Twentieth Century Fox Film Corp./Photofest
104 © Design Pics/Punchstock
107 © Photodisc/Getty Images
115 (*all*) (*Rio de Janeiro*) © John Banagan/age fotostock; (*Cairo*) © Robin Laurance/Look/age fotostock; (*Hong Kong*) © Martyn Vickery/Alamy; (*Salzburg*) © Lebrecht Music and Arts Photo Library/Alamy
118 © H.Mark Weidman Photography/Alamy
120 © Corbis flirt/Alamy
122 (*bottom row*) © Creatas Images/Thinkstock; © Chan Leong Hin/age fotostock; © Jay Newman/LWA/Blend Images/Getty Images
126 (*Heads, Tails*) © Jeffrey Kuan/iStockphoto

interchange

Jack C. Richards
Revised by Lynne Robertson

VIDEO ACTIVITY WORKSHEETS 2A

CAMBRIDGE
UNIVERSITY PRESS

Credits

Illustration credits

Andrezzinho: 22 (*bottom*), 36, 50; Ilias Arahovitis: 14 (*bottom*), 16 (*center*), 30; Ralph Butler: 4, 16 (*top*), 29, 49, 54; Carlos Diaz: 28, 48 (*top*), 52, 58; Chuck Gonzales: 12, 34 (*top*), 38 (*top*), 46 (*top*), 56 (*bottom*), 64; Jim Haynes: 24, 30, 41, 57, 62 (*bottom*); Trevor Keen: 10 (*bottom*), 20, 40, 48 (*bottom*), 56 (*top*); Joanna Kerr: 18, 34 (*bottom*); KJA-artists.com: 14 (*top*), 22 (*top*), 38 (*center*), 45, 62 (*top*); Karen Minot: 6; Ortelius Design: 42; James Yamasaki: 17

Photography credits

2 ©Radius Images/Alamy; 6 ©Glenn van der Knijff/Lonely Planet; 8 (*left to right*) ©Mark Gibson/DanitaDelimont.com"Danita Delimont Photography"/Newscom; ©Joel W. Rogers/Corbis; ©Wendy White/Alamy; ©All Canada Photos/SuperStock; 18 ©Barry Winiker/Photo Library; 20 (*left to right*) ©Jeff Greenberg/PhotoEdit; ©Ben Blankenburg/iStockphoto; ©DDP/Fotolia; 26 ©Paula Solloway/Alamy; 31 ©Jiang Hongyan/Shutterstock; ©Philip Scalia/Alamy

Video credits

Unit 7 courtesy of Allrecipes.com. Used with permission. Unit 11 courtesy of Paul Rose. Used with permission. Unit 14 courtesy of bnet.com. Used with permission.

Plan of Video 2A

1 What do you miss most?

1 CULTURE

The United States is a country of immigrants. Until the 1960s, most immigrants came from Europe. Today, most come from Latin America and Asia, but there are some immigrants from almost every country in the world. In Virginia, one high school has students from 85 countries. In Sacramento, California, at one elementary school over 50% of the students speak a language other than English at home. In both schools, the school lunch program offers foods from many countries, and most students have friends from different cultures. Still, students get homesick. "I like it here, but sometimes I miss what I left behind," says Ji Eun Park, a South Korean immigrant to New York.

Are there immigrants in your country? Where are they from?
Do you have friends in other countries? Which countries?
What do you think immigrants miss? Name two things.

2 VOCABULARY *Life in a new place*

PAIR WORK Put three more items in each column. (Many can go in both columns.) Then compare around the class.

architecture	friends	nature	sports
✓ family gatherings	holidays	professions	traditions
food	music and dance	✓ skills	

Things immigrants bring with them	Things immigrants miss
skills	family gatherings

3 GUESS THE FACTS

Watch the video with the sound off. Where are these people from? What is it like there?

4 GET THE PICTURE

Complete the chart. Fill in each person's country of origin. Then add one more piece of information. Compare with a partner.

First name:
Nami

Country:
Syria

Other:
used to play soccer

First name:
Patricia

Country:

Other:

First name:
Rolando

Country:

Other:

First name:
Mihoko

Country:

Other:

5 WATCH FOR DETAILS

Check (✓) **True** or **False**. Then correct the false statements. Compare with a partner.

	True	False	
1. Joon was born in North America.	☐	✓	Joon was born in South Korea.
2. Joon moved when she was 18.	☐	☐	
3. Nami used to play soccer in Syria.	☐	☐	
4. Nami misses spending time with his brother.	☐	☐	
5. Patricia came to the U.S. when she was 19.	☐	☐	
6. Patricia's parents miss having family around.	☐	☐	
7. Rolando used to listen to music in English.	☐	☐	
8. Rolando used to work for a record company.	☐	☐	
9. Mihoko has been in the U.S. for 6 years.	☐	☐	
10. Mihoko studied art in New York.	☐	☐	

6 WHAT DO THEY REMEMBER?

What do these people remember most about their home countries?
Check (✓) all the correct answers. Then compare with a partner.

	1 Nami	**2** Patricia	**3** Rolando	**4** Mihoko
family	✓	☐	☐	☐
food	☐	☐	☐	☐
going to the beach	☐	☐	☐	☐
listening to music in English	☐	☐	☐	☐
parties	☐	☐	☐	☐
picnics	☐	☐	☐	☐
playing soccer	✓	☐	☐	☐
restaurants	☐	☐	☐	☐

≡ Follow-up

7 DIFFICULT CHOICES

A **GROUP WORK** Imagine you're going to move to a
new country. Add two questions to the list. Then
interview three classmates and complete the chart.

I'd like to move to Australia.

	Classmate 1	Classmate 2	Classmate 3
1. Which country will you choose?			
2. What will you miss most?			
3. What will your biggest problem be?			
4.			
5.			

B **CLASS ACTIVITY** Compare answers as a class.

8 WHAT DID THEY SAY?

Watch the video and complete the conversation. Then practice it.

Joon Park is interviewing Rolando, an immigrant from Mexico.

Joon: When you ....were........ a kid, what did you .... to do for fun?

Rolando: Most of the ...., I have to say, that I used .... listen to .... in English. I used to listen to .... over and over and over.

Joon: What .... you use to do for .... in Mexico?

Rolando: I used to work for a record ....

Joon: What was it ...., moving to the United States?

Rolando: In the beginning, it was .... not to be able to communicate and .... to people and make .... understood, and .... I felt, um, frustrated a .... of times. But once my English ...., I was able to communicate ....

Joon: What do you .... most about your .... country?

Rolando: Besides my ...., the food. The food is .... in Mexico. It's .... colorful.

9 PAST TENSE QUESTIONS *Finding out about someone*

A Complete the questions with the phrases in the box. Then add two questions of your own.

1. Where _were you born_ .... ?
2. How many .... ?
3. Did you play .... ?
4. Where did you .... ?
5. Did you study .... ?
6. Did you work .... ?
7. .... ?
8. .... ?

> any sports in high school
> English in high school
> go to high school
> ✓were you born
> part-time after school
> people are in your family

B **PAIR WORK** Interview a classmate. Take turns asking and answering the questions.

2 Victoria, British Columbia

1 CULTURE

Victoria, British Columbia, is located on the tip of Vancouver Island. It is the capital city of the province of British Columbia, Canada. Victoria started as a port in the 1800s. There were many beautiful buildings then, and most of them are still standing today. Victoria has a mild climate and is very sunny – good conditions for growing a wide variety of plants. Its nickname is "The City of Gardens." Victoria is a popular place for tourists now. Many people take the ferry from the city of Vancouver (which is not on the island) to visit Victoria. Popular sites include the Empress Hotel and Beacon Hill Park.

Would you like to visit Victoria?
What other interesting facts do you know about Canada?

2 VOCABULARY Locations

PAIR WORK Imagine that you are visiting Victoria. Ask about the location of places to see. Use the map and some of these words.

across from	between	near	straight ahead
behind	just past	not far from	to the right/left

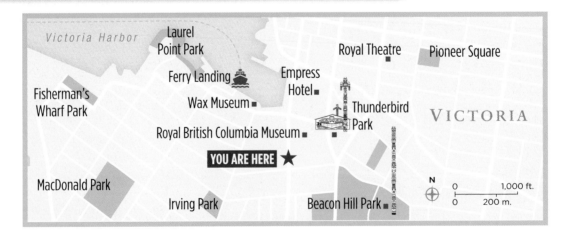

A: Excuse me. Do you know where Thunderbird Park is?
B: It's not far from the Empress Hotel.

3 GUESS THE STORY

Watch the first two minutes of the video with the sound off.
These people are taking a tour of Victoria. What do you think
the problem is? Check (✓) your answer.

☐ The tour guide gets lost.
☐ Someone on the tour is too talkative.
☐ The tour guide doesn't know the answers to questions.
☐ One of the tourists falls asleep.
☐ The tourists don't like Victoria.

☰ Watch the video

4 GET THE PICTURE

A Look at your answer to Exercise 3. Did you guess correctly?

B Check (✓) the things the tour group did. Then compare
with a partner.

☑ They took pictures of the Empress Hotel.
☐ They took a tour inside the Royal British Columbia Museum.
☐ They went to Thunderbird Park.
☐ They ate lunch in Vancouver.
☐ They visited Craigdarroch Castle.
☐ They stopped at Beacon Hill Park.

5 WATCH FOR DETAILS

What did you learn about Victoria? Check (✓) the
correct answers. Then compare with a partner.

1. A room at the Empress Hotel
   ☐ opened in 1907.
   ☑ costs more than 300 Canadian dollars.

2. The totem poles at Thunderbird Park are from
   ☐ the first people who lived in the area.
   ☐ Vancouver.

3. Craigdarroch Castle is known for
   ☐ its famous guests.
   ☐ its stained-glass windows.

4. The totem pole in Beacon Hill Park is
   ☐ not the original one.
   ☐ the fourth tallest in the world.

6 WHAT'S YOUR OPINION?

A **PAIR WORK** Check (✓) the words that describe Ted.
Can you add two words of your own?

annoying	outgoing	talkative	unfriendly	....
enthusiastic	smart	tired	whiny	....

B Do you like tour groups? What are the advantages? the disadvantages?

☰ Follow-up

7 A DAY IN VICTORIA

A **PAIR WORK** Which of these things would you like to do in Victoria? Number
them from 1 (most interesting) to 4 (least interesting). Compare answers with a partner.

Stay at the Empress Hotel	**Tour the Royal British Columbia Museum**	**Visit Craigdarroch Castle**	**Ride through Beacon Hill Park**

B **GROUP WORK** Plan a morning in Victoria. Choose two things to do.

8 TOURIST INFORMATION

A **GROUP WORK** You work for the Tourist Information Center in your city.
Fill in the name of your city. Then complete the chart for visitors.

A BRIEF GUIDE TO .... *(name of city)*	*Some interesting facts*	*Buildings and landmarks* ....
	Local foods	*Interesting things to do* ....

B Now one student in your group will play the role of a curious tourist. The tourist
will ask lots of questions about the information in your chart. Try to answer all of them!

Language close-up

9 WHAT DID THEY SAY?

Watch the video and complete the conversation. Then practice it.

A tour group is sightseeing in Victoria.

Rita: This ....historic....... landmark is the Fairmont Empress .... Many
.... guests .... here, from writers, ...
and queens, to .... and actresses, to ....

Ken: .... us .... the hotel opened?

Rita: Yes, it .... in 1907.

Yuka: .... how much a room ....
for one night?

Rita: Well, the Empress is a .... hotel, so a room ....
run over ....

10 INDIRECT QUESTIONS *Asking for information*

A Change these sentences to indirect questions. Begin with **Could you tell me . . . ?** or **Do you know . . . ?**

1. What time does the tour end?   *Could you tell me what time the tour ends?*

2. Where is the Empress Hotel? ....

3. Where do the totem poles come from? ....

4. How late does the museum stay open? ....

5. When does the next ferry to Vancouver leave? ....

B **PAIR WORK** Take turns asking and answering the questions using the information from the video.

C **GROUP WORK** Now take turns asking indirect questions about other cities. How many questions can your group answer?

3 The right apartment

☰ Preview

1 CULTURE

Colleges and universities in the United States and Canada usually provide dormitories for students on campus, but almost 60 percent prefer to live in apartments with friends. In a recent survey, most students said that dormitories have too many rules. Even more said that it was just easier to live with friends. But even friends can have problems when they rent an apartment together. The biggest problems: deciding who's going to cook and clean, getting things fixed when they don't work, and living with other people's bad habits.

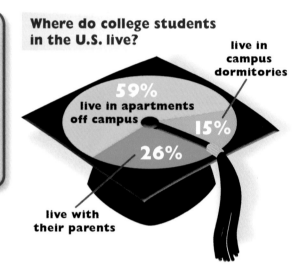

Where do college students in the U.S. live?

live in campus dormitories

59% live in apartments off campus

15%

26%

live with their parents

Where do university students usually live in your country? Why? What do you think are some advantages and disadvantages of sharing an apartment with friends?

2 VOCABULARY *Apartment hunting*

PAIR WORK What do you think are the most important factors in renting an apartment? Number the items below from 1 (most important) to 8 (least important).

appliances

location

noise

rent

security

size

view

other ....

3 GUESS THE STORY

Watch the first minute of the video with the sound off.
What don't the young women like about their apartment? Choose an answer from Exercise 2.

They don't like the ....

Watch the video

4 GET THE PICTURE

What is each apartment like? Circle the correct answers. Then compare with a partner.

Current apartment	Hudson Street apartment	Lakeview Drive apartment	Third Avenue apartment
1. big small	not near school near school	big small	less expensive more expensive
2. noisy quiet	big small	bright dark	downtown in the suburbs
3. bright dark	noisy quiet	not near school near school	big small
4. big kitchen small kitchen	bright dark	less expensive more expensive	bright dark

5 WATCH FOR DETAILS

Correct the mistakes below. Then compare with a partner.

                                                          are students

Amber, Molly, and Ellen ~~work~~ at a university, and they want to find

a new apartment. They look in the newspaper. There is a noisier

apartment for rent on Hudson Street. There is a more expensive

apartment on Lakeview Drive that has a dingy kitchen.

The apartment on Third Avenue is less expensive and has three

bedrooms. The girls decide to choose the second apartment.

Unit 3 ▪ 11

6 A MATTER OF OPINION

A Who holds these opinions? Check (✓) all the correct answers. Then compare with a partner.

	Ellen	Amber	Molly
Hudson Street apartment			
good location	☐	☐	☐
too small	☐	☐	☐
too close to school	☐	☐	☐
Lakeview Drive apartment			
too expensive	☐	☐	☐
too far from school	☐	☐	☐
much brighter	☐	☐	☐
Third Avenue apartment			
the nicest	☐	☐	☐
good location	☐	☐	☐
too small/no privacy	☐	☐	☐

B **PAIR WORK** Which apartment do you think Ellen, Amber, and Molly will choose? Why?

☰ Follow-up

7 ROLE PLAY Renting an apartment

A **PAIR WORK** Imagine that you want to rent an apartment with two friends. What questions will you need to ask? Make a list.

1. How much is the rent?
2. How many bedrooms does it have?
3. ....

4. ....
5. ....
6. ....

B **GROUP WORK** Now join another pair. Three of you are friends. The fourth person is a rental agent.

Agent: Describe two different apartments. Make them sound as different as possible.

Friends: Ask lots of questions about the two apartments.

Start like this:

Friend 1: We're looking for an apartment in *(name of neighborhood)*.
Agent: Well, I have two great apartments to show you.
Friend 2: How big are they?

Is it noisy?
Does it have a new stove?
Is it downtown?

Language close-up

8 WHAT DID THEY SAY?

Watch the video and complete the conversation. Then practice it.

The three roommates debate which apartment to choose.

Amber: I know it isn't ....*much*.... ...*bigger*.... than this place, but I like the
.... on Hudson Street. The location is .... ;
we can .... to school.

Molly: Yeah. There are three .... , but I ....
it was ....

Amber: But it's so .... ! We can walk to the ....
to study – and that .... money, too.

Ellen: But .... we .... a bigger apartment,
we .... study at the library. We
.... study at home. The apartment on Hudson Street
is .... to school. It's like .... in
a dormitory.

Molly: Yeah, that's true. But it .... noisy ....
this place, and I .... when it's ....

9 EVALUATIONS AND COMPARISONS *Giving opinions*

A Complete the sentences using **is too . . .** or **isn't . . . enough**, choosing
words from the box. Then compare with a partner. Make sure your sentences
are true in the video!

1. The roommates think their apartment ....*is too small*......... for three people.
2. Ellen thinks the apartment on Hudson Street .... to school.
3. Ellen thinks one tiny window ....
4. Amber thinks the Lakeview Drive apartment .... from school.
5. Molly thinks the Lakeview Drive apartment ....
6. Ellen and Amber think the Third Avenue apartment ....

big
bright
close
expensive
far
✓small

B Now compare two of the apartments using **as . . . as**. Share your sentences
with a partner.

1. *The old apartment isn't as big as the one on Hudson Street.*
2. ....
3. ....
4. ....
5. ....

C **PAIR WORK** Now compare your own house or apartment to one of the
apartments the roommates looked at. Do you think you would like to live there?

4 What's Cooking?

☰ Preview

1 CULTURE

Cooking in the United States and Canada is popular with both men and women. There are best-selling cookbooks and popular TV cooking shows to help people learn to cook almost every kind of food. But cooking shows appeal to people who don't like to cook, too. Some cooking shows feature chefs competing against each other (like *Iron Chef*) or exploring new foods in different countries (like *No Reservations*). And many people film their own cooking demonstrations and post them online. For North Americans, watching cooking shows isn't just educational – it's entertaining!

What do you think the programs Iron Chef *and* No Reservations *are about?*
Would you like to be on a cooking show? Why or why not?
Who likes to cook in your family?

2 VOCABULARY *Cooking*

PAIR WORK What things can you use to cook chicken? Put the words in the chart. Can you add four more words?

Kitchen appliances	Cooking utensils	Cooking ingredients
a refrigerator	a baking dish	salt
....	....	....
....	....	....
....	....	....
....	....	....

bread crumbs   butter

flour   ✓ a baking dish

a stove   ✓ salt   ✓ a refrigerator   a frying pan   an oven   oil   a knife

3 GUESS THE STORY

Answer these questions.

1. What do you think the text message says? Who do you think it's from?

2. What do the producer and the cameraman decide to do?

3. Who do you think this man is?

Watch the video

4 GET THE PICTURE

Check (✓) the correct answers. Then compare with a partner.

1. Why is Hank doing the cooking show today?
   - ☐ He has changed jobs.
   - ☐ The chef is sick.
   - ☐ He's learning to cook.

2. What does Hank usually do?
   - ☐ He's a news reporter.
   - ☐ He's a sports reporter.
   - ☐ He's a producer.

3. How successful was Hank as a chef?
   - ☐ He was very successful.
   - ☐ He was just OK.
   - ☐ He was not very successful.

5 MAKING INFERENCES

Which statements are probably true? Which are probably false?
Check (✓) your answers. Then compare with a partner.

	True	False
1. Olivia was surprised by Juliana's text message.	☐	☐
2. Hank wants to do the cooking show.	☐	☐
3. Hank has cooked Chicken con Mozzarella before.	☐	☐
4. Hank knows the difference between the microwave and the oven.	☐	☐
5. The oven is too hot.	☐	☐
6. Hank pounds the chicken correctly.	☐	☐
7. Hank uses the correct amount of salt and pepper.	☐	☐
8. Hank adds too much butter.	☐	☐
9. The producers think Hank should always host the cooking show.	☐	☐
10. Juliana will do the show next week.	☐	☐

6 A SIMPLE MEAL

A **PAIR WORK** Do you know how to make a grilled cheese sandwich?
Number the steps (1 to 6). Then practice giving instructions like this:

This is how you make a grilled cheese sandwich.

.... Finally, take the hot sandwich out of the pan, and you have
a grilled cheese sandwich.

.... Next, put some cheese between the slices of bread.

.... First, take two slices of bread.

.... After that, put the sandwich in the hot frying pan.

.... When the first side is cooked, flip the sandwich with a spatula.

.... Then heat up a frying pan with some butter or oil.

B Now write out instructions for your own simple snack, but
put the steps in the wrong order. Read the steps out loud.
Your partner will put them in the correct order.

A Quick Snack

Flour

7 HOW ABOUT YOU?

PAIR WORK Answer these questions.

1. Do you ever cook at home? Why or why not?
2. What are three dishes that you know how to make?
3. Have you ever had an accident in the kitchen? What happened?

WHAT'S THE RECIPE?

Watch the video and complete the recipe. Then compare with a partner.

Here is the recipe Hank Walker tried to follow.

Chicken con Mozzarella

First turn the .... to 350 degrees Fahrenheit.

Next, ... the chicken.

Then .... the chicken with a little salt and pepper.

Next, ... butter on the chicken.

After that, ... a strip of mozzarella cheese .... each piece of chicken. .... with a toothpick.

Now, for the coating on the ....

First, ... two eggs.

After that, ... the chicken in flour, the eggs, and bread crumbs.

Place in a .... dish.

After that, sprinkle .... rosemary.

Finally, ... the chicken in the oven and .... for 20 minutes.

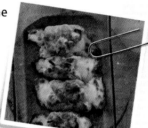

 ## SEQUENCE ADVERBS *Giving instructions*

Put the pictures in order (1 to 8). Then give the correct instructions for each photo, choosing from the verbs in the box. Use the sequence adverbs **first, then, next, after that,** and **finally.**

bake	roll
beat	spread
✓pound	sprinkle
roll	sprinkle

....
....

....
....

Finally, ...
....

....
....

1
First, pound the
chicken.

....
....

....
....

....
....

5 The great outdoors

1 *CULTURE*

Every year, millions of people in the United States and Canada go camping. Many bring tents and sleeping bags and go to a park campsite. Some go to quiet wilderness areas with few people. Others go to private campgrounds. Most people say they camp to get away from everything and everyone. But this is not always possible. At popular parks like Yellowstone National Park and the Grand Canyon, you have to make a reservation for a campsite months in advance – and be prepared for traffic jams!

Have you ever gone camping? Where? When?
What do you think are two enjoyable things and two difficult things about camping?

2 *VOCABULARY* *Camping*

PAIR WORK What would you take on a camping trip? Put the words in the chart. Can you add three more words?

Camping equipment	Food and drink	Things to enjoy
a backpack		

✓ **a backpack** **a book** **a canoe** **a fishing pole** **a flashlight**

hamburgers and hot dogs **marshmallows** **a sleeping bag** **a tent** **water**

3 GUESS THE STORY

A *Watch the video with the sound off.*
What things does the family take on the camping trip? Circle them in Exercise 2.

B The family arrives at the campsite. What do you think each family member wants to do first?

▤ Watch the video

4 GET THE PICTURE

Check (✓) **True** or **False**. Correct the false statements. Then compare with a partner.

	True	False	
1. Ed is looking forward to reading his book.	☐	☐	....
2. Ben is planning on going swimming.	☐	☐	....
3. The family is going to roast chicken later.	☐	☐	....

5 WATCH FOR DETAILS

Check (✓) the correct answers. Then compare with a partner.

1. Ed had a hard week and is looking forward
   ☑ to peace and quiet.
   ☐ to roasting peanuts.

2. Lisa wants
   ☐ to go fishing.
   ☐ to set up the tent.

3. Ben isn't excited
   ☐ to go fishing.
   ☐ to set up the tent.

4. Michelle puts Lisa's leaf
   ☐ on her door.
   ☐ in Ed's book.

5. Ben is not
   ☐ inside the tent.
   ☐ going to go fishing.

6. In the end, Ed says he's
   ☐ not going to waste time reading.
   ☐ not going to roast marshmallows.

6 GOING CAMPING

A **GROUP WORK** Plan a weekend camping trip. First, choose one of the places below or another place that you know.

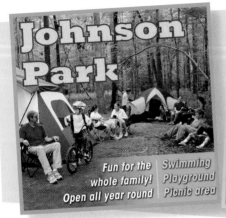

Johnson Park

Fun for the whole family! | Swimming
Open all year round | Playground | Picnic area

Rolling River
Enjoy peace and quiet!
Open April–October
Canoeing   Fishing

Mountain View
Open May–September
Sleep under the stars!
Mountain climbing
Backpacking

Now agree on answers to these questions.

1. When are we going to go?
2. How are we going to get there?
3. What are we going to take?
4. How long are we going to stay?
5. What are we going to do each day?

B **CLASS ACTIVITY** Compare your plans around the class. Which group planned the most interesting trip?

7 ROLE PLAY

A **GROUP WORK** Imagine you are a family on a camping trip. In groups of four, take the role of mother, father, or one of the two children. What would you like to do? List at least four possibilities for your character.

My character: ....

I'd like to . . .

go fishing ....

....

....

....

....

I'd like to take it easy.

B Now take turns acting out the trip: arriving at the campsite, setting up camp, and doing what you want to do. How do you get along? Who wants to do the same things? Who decides what you do?

WHAT DID THEY SAY?

Watch the video and complete the conversation. Then practice it.

Ed and Michelle arrive at the campsite with their children Ben and Lisa.

Ed: Ah, finally, some ....*peace*......... and . . .

Ben/Lisa: Sweet!! Yeah!! Cool! Awesome!

Ed: . . . .

Ben: I'm .... to .... fishing!

Lisa: I'm .... go .... the tent!

Michelle: Don't worry, Ed. .... keep an eye on them. You've had a hard week. .... don't .... grab a .... and your .... and take it easy? .... get things set up.

Ed: No, it's fine. .... I .... Lisa with the .... , and you .... go fishing with Ben.

Michelle: Uh-uh. No fishing .... camp is .... Ben!

Ben: Yeah?

Michelle: Ben, honey, ... to help your sister and father set up the .... Then you .... go fishing, OK?

Ben: Aw, Mom!

MODALS FOR SUGGESTION

A What suggestions did Michelle and Ed make? Match the phrases from columns A and B and write the sentences. Then compare with a partner.

A	B
Why don't you	read right away.
You have to	think about tonight.
Don't you think you should	help your sister and father set up the tent.
You ought to	get your sleeping bag out and get yourself set up in there?
You don't have to	grab a chair and your book and take it easy?

1. *Why don't you grab a chair and your book and take it easy?*

2. ....

3. ....

4. ....

5. ....

Why don't you take it easy?

B **PAIR WORK** Imagine that you are about to leave on a camping trip. Give five more suggestions of your own, using the expressions in column A above.

1. ....

2. ....

3. ....

4. ....

5. ....

6 What a mess!

1 CULTURE

In the United States, chores are usually divided among the members of a household. However, in a survey of married couples, 65 percent of women said that they did most of the household work. But the men did not agree. Only 5 percent of men said that the women did more work. The majority of men thought that the chores were split evenly. And what chores did men like to do? Men liked to cook dinner and clear the table. Women complained about the amount of laundry.

Who does the chores at your house? How do you decide who does what? Do you feel everyone does the same amount of work?

2 VOCABULARY Requests

A PAIR WORK What are they saying? Write one request below each picture.

Would you take out the trash?	✓ Can I use the computer now?
Could you hang up your coat, please?	Would you mind turning down the TV?
Why don't you clean up your room?	Please tell me when you're off the phone.

1. Can I use the computer now?   2. ....   3. ....

4. ....   5. ....   6. ....

B Now you make the requests. Have conversations like these:

A: Can I use the computer now?
B: Just a minute.

A: Would you take out the trash?
B: Sure. No problem.

3 GUESS THE STORY

Watch the first minute of the video with the sound off.
Answer these questions.

1. What does the daughter want?
2. What do you think her father says to her?

Watch the video

4 GET THE PICTURE

A Alexis's father asks her to do several things. Complete the sentences.
Then compare with a partner.

> go clean up your room   ✓ take out the trash
> hang up your coat   tell me what you're doing

1. Would you mind <u>taking out the trash</u> ?

2. Would you mind .... , please?

3. Would you mind .... ?

4. Why don't you .... ?

5 WATCH FOR DETAILS

Correct the mistakes below. Then compare with a partner.

Alexis comes home and greets her ~~mother~~ *father*. She asks if she can use the

telephone. Her father has to finish what he's doing, so he asks her to

cook dinner. Then he asks Alexis to order a pizza. Finally, he gives her the

computer, but he hasn't vacuumed his bookmarks or emailed the trash.

He asks Alexis to clean up the living room while he orders a salad.

6 WHAT'S YOUR OPINION?

A PAIR WORK Check (✓) the tasks you like and don't like to do.
Then compare with a partner.

	Like	Don't like
1. hang up coats	☐	☐
2. take out trash	☐	☐
3. empty trash on the computer	☐	☐
4. clean up room	☐	☐
5. put away laundry	☐	☐
6. heat up leftovers	☐	☐

B Do you sometimes get annoyed when someone you live with doesn't do
his or her chores? What kinds of things irritate you? Give opinions like this:

A: I get annoyed when my roommate turns up the TV too loud.
B: It bothers me when my brother . . .

Follow-up

7 ROLE PLAY Roommates

A PAIR WORK Imagine you have a roommate. What would you ask
him or her to do? Complete the list.

1. Would you mind vacuuming the rug?

2. ....

3. ....

B Now act out your questions with a partner.
Start like this:

A: Would you mind vacuuming the rug?
B: OK. But could you pick up your books, please?
    They're all over the floor.

8 WHAT DID THEY SAY?

Watch the video and complete the conversation. Then practice it.

Dad is working when Alexis approaches him with a request.

Dad: Would you mind ....*telling*.... ....*me*.... what you're doing?

Alexis: Nothing. . . . . the computer now?

Dad: .... it as soon as I'm finished with it.

Alexis: OK, well . . . I'm just going to .... here and wait for a while, then.

Dad: Ugh! I've got an idea: .... go clean up your room?

Alexis: I'll clean it up tonight ....

Dad: Uh-uh. You clean up your room, you .... the laptop. That's the deal.

Alexis: OK. I'll go .... now. But after that . . . ?

Dad: You can use the ....

9 TWO-PART VERBS *Making requests*

A Match each item below with at least two of the verbs in the box.
Then add three things of your own. Which of these verbs do they go with?

1. the trash	*pick up the trash*	*take out the trash*	clean up
2. your jacket	....	....	hang up
3. the TV	....	....	pick up
4. those magazines	....	....	put away
5. the laundry	....	....	take off
6.	....	....	take out
7.	....	....	turn off
8.	....	....	turn on

B **PAIR WORK** Now have conversations like these. First, use the items in part A.
Then practice the conversations again using things of your own.

A: Would you mind picking up the trash?   A: Could you take off your shoes, please?
B: Sure, no problem.   B: Yes, of course.

How to frost a cake

☰ Preview

1 CULTURE

Many cultures celebrate important occasions, like weddings or birthdays, by eating cake. The early Romans made flat round cakes sweetened with nuts and honey. In China, mooncakes are traditionally eaten during the Autumn Moon Festival. The Portuguese brought a sponge cake, *kasutera*, to Japan in the 16th century, and it is now a popular food at festivals. It seems no matter where you go, there's always an occasion for cake.

When do you eat cake? What is your favorite kind of cake?
Do you know how to make a cake?

2 VOCABULARY *Cake decorating tools*

PAIR WORK Match the words in the box with their description below. Then write the correct word under each picture.

| cake plate | ✓frosting | offset spatula | pastry brush | simple syrup | waxed paper |

frosting........................ a sweet coating used on cakes

.... a cooking tool with a bent blade used for spreading toppings

.... a small flat brush used for coating baked goods

.... a plate raised up on a platform

.... a sweet sugar liquid used to moisten cakes

.... a nonstick paper used in baking

1. ....

2. frosting.........................

3. ....

4. ....

5. ....

6. ....

3 GUESS THE FACTS

What steps are in the pictures? Choose the correct description and write it below each picture.

Make flat tops. ✓

Cut into pieces.

Spread a thin layer of frosting on the cake.

Frost, put on the top layer, and frost again.

Spread the final layer of frosting.

Apply simple syrup.

1

Make flat tops. ....

....

....

....

....

....

Place the cake on waxed paper.

Chill the cake.

Smooth the frosting.

Brush crumbs off the cake.

Smooth frosting from between the layers.

Brush on simple syrup.

....

....

....

....

....

....

☰ Watch the video

4 GET THE PICTURE

A Look at your answers to Exercise 3. Did you guess correctly? Correct your answers. Then compare with a partner.

B Put the pictures in Exercise 3 in order (1 to 6). Write the numbers in the boxes.

5 WATCH FOR DETAILS

Check (✓) **True** or **False**. Then correct the false statements. Compare with a partner.

	True	False	
1. You need to trim a rounded cake layer.	✓	☐	....
2. You use the serrated knife to spread frosting.	☐	☐	....
3. You use waxed paper to frost the cake.	☐	☐	....
4. You use simple syrup to add moisture.	☐	☐	....
5. Use a spatula to apply simple syrup.	☐	☐	....
6. It's best to try to align the cake layers.	☐	☐	....
7. A "crumb coat" is the final coat of frosting.	☐	☐	....
8. You should put the cake in the oven to chill.	☐	☐	....
9. You can use the cake plate to rotate the cake.	☐	☐	....
10. A cold spatula helps smooth the frosting.	☐	☐	....

6 HOW DOES IT WORK?

PAIR WORK Take turns describing the decorating tools shown in the video. Have conversations like this:

A: What's this?
B: It's called an offset spatula. It's used to . . .

☰ Follow-up

7 HOW TO . . .

A What is something you know how to make?
What equipment do you use? What are these things used for?
Complete the chart.

My favorite thing to make: ....
Things I use to make it	**What they're used for**
....	....
....	....
....	....
....	....

B **PAIR WORK** Take turns asking and answering questions about your chart.
Start like this:

A: What can you make?
B: I can make my own clothes.

A: What tools do you need to make them?
B: To make clothes, you need some fabric, a pattern, scissors, . . .

☰ Language close-up

8 WHAT DID SHE SAY?

Watch the video and complete the instructions. Then compare with a partner.

An expert gives instructions on how to frost a cake.

Step 1: Make flat tops. If the cake ....layers........... have domed-shaped tops, you'll .... them to make the tops flat. Place a cooled cake layer .... a sheet of .... This will make it .... to maneuver. Rest your .... on the domed top, and .... the .... parallel to the top of the cake. Lightly score the edge .... you'll make the cut. .... begin sawing .... into the cake. .... you've made one cut, ... the cake and make another cut.

9 IMPERATIVES AND INFINITIVES *Giving suggestions*

A Complete each sentence with **be sure to**, **don't forget to**, or **remember to** and one of the verbs in the box. One of the verbs can be used twice. Then compare with a partner.

align
brush
chill
hold

1. To make flat cake tops, ...remember to hold.... the knife parallel to the top of the cake.

2. When you prepare to frost, ... any loose crumbs off the cake.

3. .... a layer of simple syrup on before you frost.

4. When you place the top layer on, ... the two layers.

5. After you make the "crumb coat," .... the cake in the fridge.

B **PAIR WORK** Now describe something you are going to do. Your partner will give suggestions.

A: I'm going on a trip to Venezuela.
B: Don't forget to bring a camera.

Thanksgiving

☰ Preview

1 CULTURE

On the fourth Thursday in November, people in the United States celebrate Thanksgiving. They get together with family and friends, share a special meal, and "give thanks" for what they have. The tradition goes back to 1620, when the first group of Europeans, called Pilgrims, settled in North America. The Pilgrims didn't know how to grow crops in the New World, so the Native Americans helped them. Later, they celebrated the good harvest with a special meal. Today on Thanksgiving Day, families and friends do the very same thing.

How did the tradition of Thanksgiving begin?
Is there a similar holiday in your country? What is it?

In Canada, Thanksgiving is celebrated on the second Monday in October.

2 VOCABULARY *Thanksgiving foods*

A **PAIR WORK** Put the words in the chart. Check (✓) the ones you think are special Thanksgiving foods.

Main dishes	Side dishes	Dessert
	corn	

corn

cranberry sauce

green beans

B *Watch the first two minutes of the video with the sound off.* How many of these foods do you see? Circle them.

sweet potatoes

rolls

roast turkey with stuffing

pumpkin pie

mashed potatoes with gravy

3 GUESS THE FACTS

What do you think are the most popular Thanksgiving foods?
What do you think people do after the Thanksgiving meal?

Watch the video

4 GET THE PICTURE

Write two new things you learned about Thanksgiving.
Then compare with a partner.

NOTES

1. ....
2. ....

5 WATCH FOR DETAILS

What do these people eat on Thanksgiving? Check (✓) all the correct
answers. Then compare with a partner.

	Joe	Alisa	Susan	Juan Carlos
cranberry sauce	☐	☐	☐	☐
gravy	☐	☐	☐	☐
kimchi	☐	☐	☐	☐
maracuchitos	☐	☐	☐	☐
mashed potatoes	☐	☐	☐	☐
rice	☐	☐	☐	☐
stuffing	☐	☐	☐	☐
sweet potatoes	☐	☐	☐	☐
turkey	☐	☐	☐	☐

6 UNTRADITIONAL FOODS

Complete the sentences. Then compare with a partner.

1. Kimchi is a traditional dish from ....
2. Maracuchitos are a tradition from .... They are
   plantains with .... , fried.
3. One Venezuelan dessert is made from pineapple and .... ,
   served with ....

7 AFTER DINNER

Do Joe and Susan have these things in common? Check (✓) **True** or **False**.
Correct the false sentences. Then compare with a partner.

	True	False	
1. Joe and Susan both watch football on Thanksgiving.	☐	☐	....
2. They both spend the holiday with friends.	☐	☐	....
3. They both eat turkey, mashed potatoes, and gravy.	☐	☐	....

8 WHAT DOES THANKSGIVING MEAN TO THEM?

What did these people say about Thanksgiving? Complete the sentences.
Then compare with a partner.

It's kind of a time to ....
....
....

My favorite part of Thanksgiving
is ....
....

It is a ....
....
....

 Follow-up

9 SPECIAL HOLIDAYS

CLASS ACTIVITY What is your favorite holiday? Complete the chart. Then
compare answers as a class. How many holidays did your class list?

Name of holiday: ....

1. When is it? ....

2. What special foods do you eat? ....

3. What else do you do? ....

4. What does the holiday mean to you? ....

☰ Language close-up

10 WHAT DID THEY SAY?

Watch the video and complete the conversation. Then practice it.

A host is asking people about Thanksgiving in North America.

Host: Hello and welcome to this week's ......*episode*........ of *Dinner*
.... , the show .... food. My ....
is Anthony Russo. And .... we're ....
to be talking about Thanksgiving. As you know, North America is
a huge .... Do you think everyone
.... Thanksgiving in the same way? ....
you .... they eat the same foods? Let's ask some
people and ....

*   *   *

Host: How would you .... Thanksgiving to someone
.... of North America?

Bernie: Well, you know, Thanksgiving's a .... holiday. It's kind of
a time to sit back, ... , and . . . a little reflection on how
you .... be .... for what you have.

11 RELATIVE CLAUSES OF TIME *Describing an event*

A Rewrite these sentences with relative clauses of time. Begin with
Thanksgiving is a time when . . . . Then compare with a partner.

1. Alisa's family watches football.

   Thanksgiving is a time when Alisa's family watches football.

2. Joe helps with the clean-up.

   ....

3. Juan Carlos prepares a special Venezuelan dish called maracuchitos.

   ....

4. Susan goes out to a movie with her family.

   ....

5. Bernie gives thanks for the things that he has.

   ....

B **PAIR WORK** Take turns making statements about special days in your country,
like this:

"New Year's Eve is a time when people dance in the streets."

interchange
FOURTH EDITION

Jack C. Richards

With Jonathan Hull and Susan Proctor

Series Editor: David Bohlke

CAMBRIDGE
UNIVERSITY PRESS

WORKBOOK 2A

Contents

Credits

Illustrations

Andrezzinho: 11; **Daniel Baxter:** 28, 38, 41, 48, 88; **Carlos Diaz:** 6, 77, 94; **Jada Fitch:** 17, 42; **Tim Foley:** 22, 80; **Dylan Gibson:** 86, 92; **Chuck Gonzales:** 4, 34, 67; **Joaquin Gonzalez:** 35, 59; **Dan Hubig:** 90; **Trevor Keen:** 13, 21 (*bottom*), 55, 72, 83 (*top*); **KJA-artists:** 2, 36, 50 (*left and center*), 84, 91; **Greg Lawhun:** 16, 68, 87

Monika Melnychuk: 39 (*right*) **Karen Minot:** 10, 15, 27, 65, 89; **Ortelius Design:** 30 (*map*), 64; **Rob Schuster:** 30, 45, 51, 54, 63, 73, 83 (*bottom center*), 93; **Daniel Vasconcellos:** 19, 31, 71; **James Yamasaki:** 1, 32, 79, 85; **Rose Zgodzinski:** 18, 39 (*left*), 40, 57, 75, 78, 81; **Carol Zuber-Mallison:** 3, 9, 21(*top*), 33, 50 (*top and bottom*), 69, 87

Photos

3 © Allstar Picture Library/Alamy
5 © Denkou Images/Alamy
7 (*top, left to right*) © Glowimages/Getty Images; © Dennis MacDonald/age footstock; (*middle, left to right*) © Stacy Walsh Rosenstock/Alamy; © Bill Freeman/Alamy; (*bottom, left to right*) © Lee Snider/The Image Works; © Richard Lord/PhotoEdit
8 © Michael Dwyer/Alamy
10 (*top, left to right*) © Jane Sweeney/Robert Harding World Imagery/Corbis; © Jon Arnold Images Ltd/Alamy; © VisualHongKong/Alamy; © One-image photography/Alamy
12 © Jason O. Watson/Alamy
14 (*right, top to bottom*) © Exactostock/SuperStock; © Frank van den Bergh/iStockphoto
18 (*top right*) © Alberto Pomares/iStockphoto; (*bottom, left to right*) © Betty Johnson/Dbimages/Alamy; © Mustafa Ozer/AFP/Getty Images
20 © iStockphoto/Thinkstock
23 © Tupporn Sirichoo/iStockphoto
25 © RubberBall/SuperStock
27 (*left, top to bottom*) © Licia Rubinstein/iStockphoto; © Raga Jose Fuste/Prisma Bildagentur AG/Alamy; © Radharcimages.com/Alamy
29 © Yagi Studio/Digital Vision/Getty Images
30 (*top inset*) © iStockphoto/Thinkstock; (*middle*) © Andrey Devyatov/iStockphoto
37 (*left to right*) © i love images/Alamy; © Ricardoazoury/iStockphoto; © Erik Simonsen/Photographer's Choice/Getty Images; © Angelo Arcadi/iStockphoto; © Martyn Goddard/Corbis
43 (*right, top to bottom*) © Daniel Dempster Photography/Alamy; © Tetra Images/Getty Images
46 (*right, top to bottom*) © Glow Asia/Alamy; © David Young-Wolff/PhotoEdit
47 (*left to right*) © Eye Ubiquitous/SuperStock; © Hisham Ibrahim/Photographer's Choice/Getty Images; © Bill Bachmann/Alamy; © Brand X Pictures/Thinkstock

49 © Bettmann/Corbis
52 © Hermann Erber/LOOK Die Bildagentur der Fotografen GmbH/Alamy
54 © Bruno Perousse/age footstock
58 (*top left*) © Vadym Drobot/Shutterstock; (*middle right*) © Juan Carlos Tinjaca/Shutterstock; (*middle left*) © Alena Ozerova/Shutterstock; (*bottom right*) © Stuart Jenner/Shutterstock; (*bottom left*) © iStockphoto/Thinkstock
61 © Florian Kopp/Imagebroker/Alamy
62 (*top, left to right*) © Luciano Mortula/Shutterstock; © Anibal Trejo/Shutterstock; © Julian Love/John Warburton-Lee Photography/Alamy; (*middle, left to right*) © Bill Bachman/Alamy; © Juergen Richter/LOOK Die Bildagentur der Fotografen GmbH/Alamy; © Goran Bogicevic/Shutterstock
63 (*middle, top to bottom*) © Bernardo Galmarini/Alamy; © Ariadne Van Zandbergen/Alamy
64 © Josef Polleross/The Image Works
65 (*top right*) © Robert Landau/Surf/Corbis; (*bottom right*) © Travel Pictures/Alamy
66 © Hulton-Deutsch Collection/Historical/Corbis
69 © Globe Photos/ZUMAPRESS/NEWSCOM
70 © Han Myung-Gu/WireImage/Getty Images
73 © WALT DISNEY PICTURES/Album/NEWSCOM
74 © XPhantom/Shutterstock
75 (*top left*) © Bettmann/Corbis; (*top right*) © Sunset Boulevard/Historical/Corbis
76 © Buyenlarge/Archive Photos/Getty Images
78 © LIONSGATE/Album/NEWSCOM
82 © Mark Gibson/Danita Delimont Photography/NEWSCOM
83 (*all*) © ahmet urkac/Shutterstock
95 © Workbook Stock/Getty Images
96 © maXx images/SuperStock

A time to remember

1 *Past tense*

A Write the past tense of these verbs.

Verb	Past tense	Verb	Past tense
be	was / were	hide	_____
become	_____	laugh	_____
do	_____	lose	_____
email	_____	move	_____
get	_____	open	_____
have	_____	scream	_____

B Complete this paragraph. Use the past tense of each of the verbs in part A.

My best friend in school ___was___ Michael.
He and I _____ in Mrs. Gilbert's third-grade
class, and we _____ friends.
We often _____ crazy things in class, but I don't
think Mrs. Gilbert ever really _____ mad at us.
For example, Michael _____ a pet monkey named
Bananas. Sometimes he _____ it in Mrs. Gilbert's
desk. Later, when she _____ the
drawer, she always _____ loudly,
and the class _____ . After two
years, Michael's family _____ to another town.
We _____ each other for a few years, but then
we _____ contact. I often wonder what
he's doing now.

2 Complete the questions in this conversation.

Mary: Welcome to the building. My name's Mary Burns.

Sílvio: Hello. I'm Sílvio Mendes. It's nice to meet you.

Mary: Nice to meet you, too. Are you from around here?

Sílvio: No, I'm from Brazil.

Mary: Oh, really? _Were you born_ in Brazil?

Sílvio: No, I wasn't born there, actually. I'm originally from Portugal.

Mary: That's interesting. So, when _____ to Brazil?

Sílvio: I moved to Brazil when I was in elementary school.

Mary: Where _____ ?

Sílvio: We lived in Recife. It's a beautiful city in northeast Brazil. Then I went to college.

Mary: _____ to school in Recife?

Sílvio: No, I went to school in São Paulo.

Mary: And what _____ ?

Sílvio: Oh, I studied engineering. But I'm here to go to graduate school.

Mary: Great! When _____ ?

Sílvio: I arrived last week. I start school in three days.

Mary: Well, good luck. And sorry for all the questions!

3 Answer these questions.

1. Where were you born?

   _____

2. Did your family move when you were a child?

   _____

3. Did you have a favorite teacher in elementary school?

   _____

4. What hobbies did you have when you were a kid?

   _____

5. When did you begin to learn English?

   _____

4 *Rodrigo Santoro*

A Scan the article about Rodrigo Santoro. Where is he from? What does he do?

Rodrigo Santoro was born in 1975 in Petrópolis, near Rio de Janeiro, Brazil. As a child, he used to organize puppet performances during family vacations. When he was studying communications in college, he started acting in television soap operas, such as *Olho no Olho* in 1993 and *Hilda Furacão* in 1998.

After his success in soap operas, Santoro started acting in Brazilian films. His first big role was in *Bicho de Sete Cabeças* in 2001. The movie is about a young man who is wrongly kept in a mental hospital. For this role, he won the Best Actor Award at the Cartagena Film Festival. This success led to Hollywood. In 2003, Santoro acted in three movies: *Charlie's Angels: Full Throttle*, with Drew Barrymore; *The Roman Spring of Mrs. Stone*, with Helen Mirren; and *Love Actually*, with Hugh Grant. His performance as King Xerxes of Persia in the movie *300* was nominated as Best Villain at the MTV Movie Awards in 2007.

During this time, Santoro continued working in Brazil. In 2003, he starred in *Carandiru*, a film about a prison in São Paulo. He was nominated as Best Actor at the Prêmio Contigo Cinema for his performance in the 2007 film *Não Por Acaso*. More recently, he performed the role of President Raúl Castro of Cuba in *Che: Part Two* (2008) and that of Oriol in *There Be Dragons* (2011).

With this heavy workload, Santoro balances his life in Rio de Janeiro by reading, listening to music, and meditating. He also loves sports. In 2008, he played soccer with such international stars as Luís Figo and Alan Shearer for Soccer Aid, a charity that raises money for the United Nations Children's Fund (UNICEF). ∎

B Check (✓) True or False. For statements that are false, write the correct information.

	True	False
1. Rodrigo Santoro studied acting in college.	☐	☐
_____		
2. He won an award for his role in *Bicho de Sete Cabeças*.	☐	☐
_____		
3. He worked in Brazil before he worked in Hollywood.	☐	☐
_____		
4. He won an MTV Movie Award for the role of King Xerxes.	☐	☐
_____		
5. He always plays very similar roles.	☐	☐
_____		
6. He once played soccer for a children's charity.	☐	☐
_____		

5 Choose the correct word or phrase.

1. I used to collect ____comic books____ (hobbies / scrapbooks / comic books) when I was a kid.

2. My favorite pet was a _____ (cat / beach / crayon) called Felix.

3. We used to go to _____ (video games / summer camp / toys) during our vacations. It was really fun.

4. There was a great _____ (fish / playground / soccer) in our neighborhood. We used to go there every afternoon.

6 Look at these childhood pictures of Kate and her brother Peter. Complete the sentences using used to.

1. In the summer, Kate and Peter sometimes ____used to go to summer camp.____

2. They also _____ . Their dog Bruno always used to follow them.

3. Kate _____ every weekend during summer vacation. She hardly ever goes now.

4. Peter _____ . They're now worth a lot of money.

5. They _____ . They don't have any pets now.

7 *Look at the answers. Write the questions using* used to.

1. A: <u>What did you use to do in the summer?</u>

   B: We used to go to the beach.

2. A: _____

   B: No, we didn't collect shells. We used to build sand castles.

3. A: _____

   B: Yes, we did. We used to swim for hours. Then we played all

   kinds of sports.

4. A: Really? What _____

   B: Well, we used to play beach volleyball with some other kids.

5. A: _____

   B: No, we didn't. We used to win!

8 *How have you changed in the last five years? Write answers to these questions.*

1. What hobbies did you use to have five years ago? What hobbies do you
   have now?

   <u>I used to . . .</u> _____

   <u>Now, . . .</u> _____

2. What kind of music did you use to like then? What kind of music do
   you like now?

   _____

   _____

3. What kinds of clothes did you use to like to wear? What kinds of clothes
   do you like to wear now?

   _____

   _____

A time to remember ▪ 5

9 *Complete the sentences. Use the past tense of the verbs given.*

Maria: I'm an immigrant here.

I ___was___ (be) born in Chile

and _____ (grow up) there.

I _____ (come) here in 2005.

I _____ (not be) very happy at

first. Things _____ (be) difficult

for me. I _____ (not speak)

English, so I _____ (go) to a

community college and _____ (study)

English there. My English _____ (get)

better, and I _____ (find)

this job. What about you?

10 *Choose the correct responses.*

1. A: Are you from Toronto?

   B: No, I'm originally from Morocco.

   • No, I'm originally from Morocco.
   • Neither am I.

2. A: Tell me a little about yourself.

   B: _____

   • Sure. Nice to meet you.
   • What do you want to know?

3. A: How old were you when you moved here?

   B: _____

   • About 16.
   • About 16 years ago.

4. A: Did you learn English here?

   B: _____

   • Yes, I was 10 years old.
   • No, I studied it in Morocco.

5. A: By the way, I'm Lisa.

   B: _____

   • What's your name?
   • Glad to meet you.

2 Caught in the rush

1 *Choose the correct compound noun for each picture.*

☐ bicycle lane	☐ newsstand	☐ taxi stand
☐ bus stop	☑ streetlights	☐ traffic jam

1. <u>streetlights</u>

2. _____

3. _____

4. _____

5. _____

6. _____

2 Problems, problems

A Choose a solution for each problem.

Problems

1. no more parking spaces: <u>build a public parking garage</u>

2. dark streets: _____

3. no places to take children: _____

4. crime: _____

5. car accidents: _____

6. traffic jams: _____

Solutions
☐ install modern streetlights
☐ build a subway system
☐ install more traffic lights
☐ hire more police officers
☐ build more parks
☑ build a public parking garage

B Look at these solutions. Write sentences explaining the problems.
Use *too much, too many,* or *not enough* and the problems in part A.

1. <u>There aren't enough parking spaces.</u>

   The city should build a public parking garage.

2. _____

   The city should install more traffic lights.

3. _____

   The city should build a subway system.

4. _____

   The city should hire more police officers.

5. _____

   The city should build more parks.

6. _____

   The city should install modern streetlights.

C Find another way to say the problems in part B. Begin each
sentence with *There should be more/less/fewer . . . .*

1. <u>There should be more parking spaces.</u>
2. _____
   _____
3. _____
   _____
4. _____
   _____
5. _____
   _____
6. _____
   _____

3 City blues

A Match the words in columns A and B. Write the compound nouns.

A	B	
☑ air	☐ district	1. _air pollution_
☐ business	☐ garages	2. _____
☐ commuter	☐ hour	3. _____
☐ parking	☐ lines	4. _____
☐ police	☐ officers	5. _____
☐ public	☑ pollution	6. _____
☐ rush	☐ transportation	7. _____

B Complete this online post using the compound nouns in part A.

HOME HEADLINES LOCAL NEWS INTERNATIONAL BUSINESS SPORTS CONTACT US

City Forum

Life in this city needs to be improved. For one thing, there are too many cars, and there is too much bad air, especially during _____ rush hour _____ . The _____ is terrible. This problem is particularly bad downtown in the _____ . Too many people drive their cars to work.

I think there should be more _____ at busy intersections. They could stop traffic jams. We also need fewer _____ downtown. The city spends too much money building them. It's so easy to park that too many people drive to work. However, the city doesn't spend enough money on _____ . There aren't enough _____ to the suburbs.

C Write two paragraphs about a problem in a city you know. First describe the problem and then suggest solutions.

_____

_____

_____

_____

_____

_____

_____

_____

4 *Transportation in Hong Kong*

A Read about transportation in Hong Kong. Match the photos to the descriptions in the article.

cable railway

ferry

subway

tram

Getting Around Hong Kong

✈ **Hong Kong has an excellent transportation system. If you fly there, you will arrive at one of the most modern airports in the world. And during your visit, there are many ways to get around Hong Kong.**

1 _____

These have run in the streets of Hong Kong Island since 1904. They have two decks, and they carry 230,000 passengers a day. You can travel on six routes, totaling 30 kilometers (about 19 miles). You can also hire one for a private party with up to 25 guests – a great way to enjoy Hong Kong!

2 _____

Take one of these to cross from Hong Kong Island to Kowloon or to visit one of the other islands. You can also use them to travel to Macau and Guangdong. They are very safe and comfortable, and one of the cheapest boat rides in the world.

3 _____

Hong Kong's underground railway is called the MTR – the Mass Transit Railway. It is the fastest way to get around. You can catch one from the airport to all the major centers in Hong Kong. The MTR carries 2.3 million passengers a day.

4 _____

This is found on Hong Kong Island. It pulls you up Victoria Peak, which is 552 meters (about 1,800 feet) above sea level, the highest mountain on the island. The system is over 120 years old. In that time, there has never been an accident. Two cars carry up to 120 passengers each.

B Complete the chart about each type of transportation. Where you cannot find the information, write *NG* (not given).

	cable railway	ferry	subway	tram
1. How old is it?	_____	_____	_____	_____
2. How many people use it?	_____	_____	_____	_____
3. How safe is it?	_____	_____	_____	_____
4. Where can you go?	_____	_____	_____	_____

5 Complete these conversations. Use the words in the box.

☐ ATM   ☑ duty-free shop   ☐ sign
☐ bus stop   ☐ schedule

AIRPORT INFORMATION

1. A: Could you tell me where I can buy some perfume?
   B: You should try the _duty-free shop_ .

2. A: Can you tell me where the buses are?
   B: Yeah, there's a _____ just outside this building.

3. A: Do you know where I can change money?
   B: There's a money exchange on the second floor. There's also an _____ over there.

4. A: Do you know what time the last train leaves for the city?
   B: No, but I can check the _____ .

5. A: Could you tell me where the taxi stand is?
   B: Sure. Just follow that _____ .

6 Complete the questions in this conversation at a hotel.

Guest: Could you _tell me where the gym is_ ?

Clerk: Sure, the gym is on the nineteenth floor.

Guest: OK. And can you _____ ?

Clerk: Yes, the coffee shop is next to the gift shop.

Guest: The gift shop? Hmm. I need to buy something for my wife.
       Do you _____ ?

Clerk: It closes at 6:00 P.M. I'm sorry, but you'll have to wait until tomorrow. It's already 6:15.

Guest: OK. Oh, I'm expecting a package.
       Could you _____ ?

Clerk: Don't worry. I'll call you when it arrives.

Guest: Thanks. Just one more thing.
       Do you _____ ?

Clerk: The airport bus leaves every half hour. Anything else?

Guest: No, I don't think so. Thanks.

7 *Rewrite these sentences. Find another way to say each sentence using the words given.*

1. There are too many cars in this city. (fewer)

   There should be fewer cars in this city.

2. We need fewer buses and cars downtown. (traffic)

   _____

3. Where's the subway station? (Could you)

   _____

4. There isn't enough public parking. (parking garages)

   _____

5. How often does the bus come? (Do you)

   _____

6. What time does the last train leave? (Can you)

   _____

8 *Answer these questions about your city or another city you know.*

The streets are closed to cars in a traffic-free zone.

1. Are there any traffic-free zones? If so, where are they located?

   _____

2. How do most people travel to and from work?

   _____

3. What's the rush hour like?

   _____

4. What's the city's biggest problem?

   _____

5. What has the city done about it?

   _____

6. Is there anything else the city could do?

   _____

Time for a change!

1 Opposites

A Write the opposites. Use the words in the box.

> ☐ dark   ☐ old
> ☐ expensive   ☐ safe
> ☑ inconvenient   ☐ small
> ☐ noisy   ☐ spacious

1. convenient / _inconvenient_   5. bright / _____
2. cramped / _____   6. modern / _____
3. dangerous / _____   7. quiet / _____
4. big / _____   8. cheap / _____

B Rewrite these sentences. Find another way to say each sentence using *not . . . enough* or *too* and the words in part A.

1. The house is too expensive.

   The house isn't cheap enough.

2. The rooms aren't bright enough.

   _____

3. The living room isn't spacious enough for the family.

   _____

4. The bathroom is too old.

   _____

5. The yard isn't big enough for our pets.

   _____

6. The street is too noisy for us.

   _____

7. The neighborhood is too dangerous.

   _____

8. The location isn't convenient enough.

   _____

2 *Add the word* enough *to these sentences.*

Grammar note: enough

Enough *comes* <u>after</u> *adjectives but* <u>before</u> *nouns.*
adjective + enough   **enough + noun**
It isn't *spacious enough.*   There isn't *enough space.*
The rooms aren't *light enough.*   It doesn't have *enough light.*

                                        enough

1. The apartment isn't comfortable.   5. The neighborhood doesn't have streetlights.

2. There aren't bedrooms.   6. There aren't closets.

3. It's not modern.   7. It's not private.

4. There aren't parking spaces.   8. The living room isn't spacious.

3 *Complete this conversation. Use the words given and the comparisons in the box.*
(Some of the comparisons in the box can be used more than once.)

almost as . . . as   just as many . . . as
as many . . . as   not as . . . as

Realtor: How did you like the house on Twelfth Street?

Client: Well, it's   <u>not as convenient as</u>   the apartment
on Main Street. (convenient)

Realtor: That's true, the house is less convenient.

Client: And the apartment doesn't have

_____ the house. (rooms)

Realtor: Yes, the house is more spacious.

Client: But I think there are _____

in the apartment. (closets)

Realtor: You're right. The closet space is the same.

Client: The wallpaper in the apartment is _____

_____ the wallpaper in the house. (shabby)

Realtor: I know, but you could change the wallpaper in the house.

Client: Hmm, the rent on the apartment is _____

_____ the rent on the house, but the

house is much bigger. (expensive) Oh, I can't decide.

Can you show me something else?

4 *Home, sweet home*

A Complete this questionnaire about where you live, and find your score below.

How does your home measure up?

The outside	Yes	No	To score:
1. Are you close enough to shopping?	☐	☐	How many "Yes" answers do you have?
2. Is there enough public transportation nearby?	☐	☐	
3. Are the sidewalks clean?	☐	☐	**16–20**
4. Are there good restaurants in the neighborhood?	☐	☐	It sounds like a dream home!
5. Is there a park nearby?	☐	☐	
6. Is the neighborhood quiet?	☐	☐	**11–15**
7. Is the neighborhood safe?	☐	☐	Great! All you need now is a swimming pool!
8. Is there enough parking nearby?	☐	☐	
9. Does the outside of your home look good?	☐	☐	

6–10
Well, at least guests won't want to stay too long!

The inside			
10. Are there enough bedrooms?	☐	☐	
11. Is there enough closet space?	☐	☐	**0–5**
12. Is the bathroom modern?	☐	☐	Time to look for a better place to live!
13. Is there a washing machine?	☐	☐	
14. Is there enough space in the kitchen?	☐	☐	
15. Do the stove and refrigerator work well?	☐	☐	
16. Is the living room comfortable enough?	☐	☐	
17. Is the dining area big enough?	☐	☐	
18. Are the walls newly painted?	☐	☐	
19. Are the rooms bright enough?	☐	☐	
20. Is the building warm enough in cold weather?	☐	☐	

B Write two short paragraphs about where you live. In the first paragraph describe your neighborhood, and in the second paragraph describe your home. Use the information in part A or your own information.

_____

_____

_____

_____

_____

_____

_____

_____

5 *Wishes*

A Which words or phrases often go with which verbs? Complete the chart.

☐ Italian ☐ happier ☐ my own room ☐ karate
☐ more free time ☑ healthy ☐ somewhere else ☐ to a new place

be	know	have	move
<u>healthy</u>			

B Describe what these people would like to change. Use *I wish* and words or phrases in part A.

1. <u>I wish I were healthy.</u>

2. _____

3. _____

4. _____

5. _____

6. _____

6 *Choose the correct responses.*

1. A: I wish I had an easier life.

   B: <u>Why?</u>

   - Why?
   - I don't like my job, either.

2. A: I wish I could retire.

   B: _____

   - I don't like it anymore.
   - I know what you mean.

3. A: Where do you want to move?

   B: _____

   - Somewhere else.
   - Something else.

4. A: I wish I could find a bigger apartment.

   B: _____

   - Is it too large?
   - It's very nice, though.

7 *Rewrite these sentences. Find another way to say each sentence using the words given.*

1. There should be more bedrooms in my apartment. (enough)

   <u>There aren't enough bedrooms in my apartment.</u>

2. This neighborhood is safe enough. (dangerous)

   _____

3. My apartment doesn't have enough privacy. (private)

   _____

4. Our house has the same number of bedrooms as yours. (just as many)

   _____

5. I don't have enough closet space. (wish)

   _____

6. We wish we could move to a new place. (somewhere else)

   _____

7. That apartment is too small. (big)

   _____

8. I wish housework were easy. (not difficult)

   _____

A Scan the article about making wishes. Which three countries does it refer to?

Making *Wishes*

All over the world, people have always wished for things, such as peace, love, good health, and money. Over hundreds of years, people in different countries have found different ways to make wishes. Here are some interesting examples.

The Trevi Fountain in Rome, Italy, is a place where many people go to make a wish. The water from the fountain flows into a large pool of water below. To make a wish, visitors stand facing away from the fountain. Then, they use their right hand to throw a coin into the pool over their left shoulder. They believe this will bring them luck and bring them back to Rome one day. The coins in the fountain, several thousand euros each day, are given to poor people.

A very different way of making wishes happens in Anhui province in eastern China. Huangshan (which means "Yellow Mountain") is famous for its beautiful sunrises and sunsets. That's why people think it is a very romantic place. Couples go there to make a wish that they will stay together forever. Each couple buys a "love lock," or padlock, with a key. Next, they lock their padlock to a chain at the top of the mountain. Then they throw the key down the mountain so that their lock can never be opened.

In Turkey and some neighboring countries, May 5 is a special day for making wishes. People believe that each year on that day two wise men return to earth. They come to help people and give them good health. In the evening, there are street food markets selling different kinds of seasonal food and musicians playing traditional music. People write their wishes on pieces of paper and then attach the paper to a tree. Nowadays, however, some people go online and send their wishes to special websites.

B Read the article. Check (✓) the statements that are true for each place.

	Rome	Huangshan	Turkey
1. People make wishes only once a year.	☐	☐	☐
2. You need a lock and key.	☐	☐	☐
3. You put your wish on a tree.	☐	☐	☐
4. You need a coin to make your wish.	☐	☐	☐
5. Wish-making is only for couples.	☐	☐	☐
6. The money from the wishes goes to poor people.	☐	☐	☐
7. Some people make their wishes on the Internet.	☐	☐	☐

I've never heard of that!

1 **Complete the conversation with the correct tense.**

Isabel: I went to Sunrise Beach last week.

<u>Have you ever been</u>
(Did you ever go / Have you ever been)

to Sunrise Beach, Andy?

Andy: Yes, _____ . It's beautiful.
(I did / I have)

_____ there on
(Did you go / Have you gone)

the weekend?

Isabel: Yeah, I _____ .
(did / have)

I _____ on Sunday.
(went / have gone)

_____ at 4:00 A.M.
(I got up / I've gotten up)

Andy: Wow! _____ that early!
(I never woke up / I've never woken up)

Isabel: Oh, it wasn't so bad. I _____
(got / have gotten)

to the beach early to see the sun come up.

_____ a sunrise on a beach, Andy?
(Did you ever see / Have you ever seen)

Andy: No, _____ .
(I didn't / I haven't)

Isabel: Then I _____ swimming
(went / have gone)

around 6:00, but there were some strange dark shadows

in the water. _____ of sharks at Sunrise Beach?
(Did you ever hear / Have you ever heard)

Andy: Yes, _____ . I _____ a news report about sharks last summer.
(I did / I have)   (heard / have heard)

Isabel: Gee! Maybe I _____ a lucky escape on Sunday morning! Why don't you
(had / have had)

come with me next time?

Andy: Are you kidding?

2 *Have you ever ... ?*

A Look at this list and check (✓) five things you have done. Add other activities if necessary.

- ☐ go horseback riding
- ☐ cook for over 10 people
- ☐ eat raw fish
- ☐ go to a classical concert
- ☐ have green tea ice cream
- ☐ read a novel in English
- ☐ ride a motorcycle
- ☐ take a cruise
- ☐ travel abroad
- ☐ try Indian food
- ☐ _____
- ☐ _____
- ☐ _____
- ☐ _____

B Write questions about the things you checked in part A. Use *Have you ever ... ?*

1. Have you ever had green tea
   ice cream?
2. _____
   _____
3. _____
   _____
4. _____
   _____
5. _____
   _____

C Answer the questions you wrote in part B. Then use the past tense to give more information.

1. Yes, I have. I had some in a
   Japanese restaurant. It was delicious!
2. _____
   _____
3. _____
   _____
4. _____
   _____
5. _____
   _____

3 Do I have a food allergy?

A Scan the article. What kinds of food can cause allergies?

FOOD ALLERGIES

Luis always had headaches and stomachaches. First, Luis's doctor gave him some medicine, but it didn't work. Then his doctor asked him about his favorite foods. Luis said he loved cake and ice cream. His doctor said, "Stop eating sweets." Luis stopped, but he still got headaches and stomachaches. Next, his doctor asked more questions about his diet. Luis said he ate a lot of fish. His doctor said to stop eating fish. When Luis stopped eating fish, he felt much better.

Sharon often had a very sore mouth after eating. First, she stopped drinking milk and eating cheese, but this made no difference. Then, in the summer, the problem became really bad, and it was difficult for Sharon to eat. Her doctor asked about her diet. She said she had a tomato garden, and she ate about 10 tomatoes a day. Sharon's doctor told her not to eat tomatoes. When she stopped eating tomatoes, Sharon's mouth got better.

Fred is a mechanic, but he was not able to hold his tools. His hands were swollen. First, he went to his doctor, and she gave him some medicine. The medicine didn't work. He still couldn't hold his tools. After that, his doctor asked him about his diet. Fred told her he ate a lot of bread. She told him not to eat bread or pasta. After 10 days, Fred could hold his tools again.

B Read the article. What problem did each person have? Complete the first column of the chart.

	Problem	What didn't work	What worked
Luis	_____	_____	_____
Sharon	_____	_____	_____
Fred	_____	_____	_____

C Read the article again. What didn't work? What *did work*? Complete the rest of the chart.

Eggs, anyone?

A Here's a recipe for a mushroom omelet. Look at the pictures and number the sentences from 1 to 5.

_____ After that, pour the eggs into a frying pan. Add the mushrooms and cook.

_____ Then beat the eggs in a bowl.

__1__ First, slice the mushrooms.

_____ Next, add salt and pepper to the egg mixture.

_____ Finally, fold the omelet in half. Your omelet is ready. Enjoy!

B Describe your favorite way to cook eggs. Use sequence adverbs.

How to cook: _____

5 Complete the conversation. Use the past tense or the present perfect of the verbs given.

Sylvia: I ____went____ (go) to a Thai restaurant last night.

Jason: Really? I _____ (never eat) Thai food.

Sylvia: Oh, you should try it. It's delicious!

Jason: What _____ you _____ (order)?

Sylvia: First, I _____ (have) soup with green curry and

rice. Then I _____ (try) pad thai. It's noodles,

shrimp, and vegetables in a spicy sauce.

Jason: I _____ (not taste) pad thai before. _____ (be)

it very hot?

Sylvia: No. It _____ (be) just spicy enough. And after

that, I _____ (eat) bananas in coconut milk

for dessert.

Jason: Mmm! That sounds good.

Sylvia: It was.

6 Choose the correct word.

1. We had delicious guacamole dip and chips on Saturday night while we watched TV.

It was a great ____snack____ (dinner / snack / meal).

2. I had a huge lunch, so I _____ (ordered / skipped / tried) dinner.

3. What _____ (appetizers / ingredients / skewers) do

you need to cook crispy fried noodles?

4. First, fry the beef in oil and curry powder and then _____

(pour / mix / toast) the coconut milk over the beef.

5. We need to leave the restaurant now. Could we have the

_____ (check / recipe / menu), please?

7 Choose the correct responses.

> ☐ Yuck! That sounds awful. ☐ That sounds strange. ☐ Mmm! That sounds good.

1. A: Have you ever tried barbecued chicken? You marinate the meat
   in barbecue sauce for about an hour and then cook it on the grill.

   B: _____

2. A: Here's a recipe called Baked Eggplant Delight. I usually bake eggplant for
   an hour, but this says you bake it for only five minutes!

   B: _____

3. A: Look at this dish – frogs' legs with bananas! I've never seen that before.

   B: _____

8 Crossword puzzle: Verbs

Use the simple past or present perfect of these verbs to complete the crossword puzzle.

> ☑ be   ☐ bring   ☐ decide   ☐ drive   ☐ forget   ☐ have   ☐ ride   ☐ take
> ☐ break ☐ buy   ☐ do   ☐ eat   ☐ give   ☐ make   ☐ skip   ☐ try

Across

1 We have never _____ to a Chinese restaurant.

3 I _____ all the ingredients with me.

7 _____ you eat a huge dinner last night?

8 We _____ my mother to the new Chilean restaurant.

11 I haven't _____ a birthday gift to my father yet.

12 Have you ever _____ a horse? It's great!

13 I have never _____ snails. What are they like?

14 Have you _____ what kind of pizza you would like?

Down

1 I _____ this chicken for $5.

2 Oh, I'm sorry. I just _____ a glass.

4 Victor _____ Chinese chicken for dinner.

5 I wasn't hungry this morning, so I _____ breakfast.

6 Oh, no! I _____ to buy rice.

7 Have you ever _____ a sports car?

9 I _____ Greek food for the first time last night.

10 Have you ever _____ Peruvian ceviche? It's delicious.

5 Going places

Vacation plans

A Which words or phrases often go with which verbs?
Complete the chart. Use each word or phrase only once.

- ☐ a camper
- ☐ camping
- ☐ a car
- ☐ a condominium
- ☑ long walks

- ☐ lots of hiking
- ☐ my email
- ☐ my reading
- ☐ my studying
- ☐ on vacation

- ☐ sailing lessons
- ☐ some fishing
- ☐ something exciting
- ☐ swimming
- ☐ a vacation

take	do	go
long walks		

rent	catch up on

B Write four things you plan to do on your next vacation. Use *be going to* and the information in part A or your own information.

Vacation plans

1. _____
2. _____
3. _____
4. _____

C Write four sentences about your possible vacation plans. Use *will* with *maybe*, *probably*, *I guess*, or *I think*. Use the information in part A or your own information.

Possible plans

1. _____
2. _____
3. _____
4. _____

2 *Complete the conversation. Use* **be going to** *or* **will** *and the information on the notepads.*

Dave: So, Stella, do you have any vacation plans?

Stella: Well, <u>I'm going to paint my apartment</u> because the walls are a really ugly color. What about you?

Dave: _____ and take a long drive.

Stella: Where are you going to go?

Dave: I'm not sure. _____ . I haven't seen her in a long time.

Stella: That sounds nice. I like to visit my family, too.

Dave: Yes, and _____ for a few days. I haven't been hiking in months. How about you? Are you going to do anything else on your vacation?

Stella: _____ . I have a lot of work to do before school starts.

Dave: That doesn't sound like much fun.

Stella: Oh, I am planning to have some fun, too. _____ . I love to swim in the ocean!

Stella's Pad

paint my apartment - yes

catch up on my studying - probably

relax on the beach - yes

DAVE'S PAD

rent a car - yes

visit my sister Joanne - probably

go to the mountains - maybe

3 *Travel plans*

A Look at these answers. Write questions using *be going to.*

1. A: <u>Where are you going to go?</u>

   B: I'm going to go someplace nice and quiet.

2. A: _____

   B: I'm going to drive.

3. A: _____

   B: I'm going to stay in a condominium. My friend has one near the beach.

4. A: _____

   B: No, I'm going to travel by myself.

B Use the cues to write other answers to the questions in part A. Use *be going to* or *will*.

1. <u>I'm not going to go to a busy place.</u> (not go / busy place)

2. _____ (maybe / take the train)

3. _____ (not stay / hotel)

4. _____ (I think / ask a friend)

Travel ads

A Scan the travel ad. Where can tourists see beautiful nature scenes?

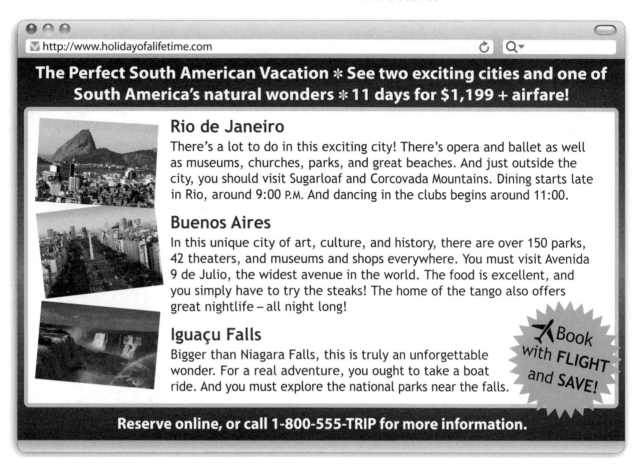

http://www.holidayofalifetime.com

The Perfect South American Vacation ✳ See two exciting cities and one of South America's natural wonders ✳ 11 days for $1,199 + airfare!

Rio de Janeiro

There's a lot to do in this exciting city! There's opera and ballet as well as museums, churches, parks, and great beaches. And just outside the city, you should visit Sugarloaf and Corcovada Mountains. Dining starts late in Rio, around 9:00 P.M. And dancing in the clubs begins around 11:00.

Buenos Aires

In this unique city of art, culture, and history, there are over 150 parks, 42 theaters, and museums and shops everywhere. You must visit Avenida 9 de Julio, the widest avenue in the world. The food is excellent, and you simply have to try the steaks! The home of the tango also offers great nightlife – all night long!

Iguaçu Falls

Bigger than Niagara Falls, this is truly an unforgettable wonder. For a real adventure, you ought to take a boat ride. And you must explore the national parks near the falls.

✈Book with FLIGHT and SAVE!

Reserve online, or call 1-800-555-TRIP for more information.

B Read the ad. Check (✓) True or False. For the statements that are false, write the correct information.

	True	False
1. People have dinner late in Rio de Janeiro.	☐	☐
2. Buenos Aires has the longest avenue in the world.	☐	☐
3. Niagara Falls is bigger than Iguaçu Falls.	☐	☐
4. Both Rio de Janeiro and Buenos Aires have exciting nightlife.	☐	☐
5. Rio de Janeiro, Buenos Aires, and Iguaçu Falls have unforgettable parks and beaches.	☐	☐

5 Circle the correct word or words to give advice to travelers.

1. You ought (check / to check) the weather.
2. You should never (leave / to leave) cash in your hotel room.
3. You need (take / to take) your credit card with you.
4. You have (pay / to pay) an airport tax.
5. You should (let / to let) your family know where they can contact you.
6. You'd better not (go / to go) out alone late at night.
7. You must (get / to get) a vaccination if you go to some countries.

6 Take it or leave it?

A Check (✓) the most important item to have in each situation.

1. A vacation to a foreign country
   - ☐ an overnight bag
   - ✓ a passport
   - ☐ a driver's license

2. A mountain-climbing vacation
   - ☐ a suitcase
   - ☐ a visa
   - ☐ hiking boots

3. A sailing trip
   - ☐ a hotel reservation
   - ☐ a first-aid kit
   - ☐ an ATM card

4. A visit to a temple
   - ☐ a credit card
   - ☐ suitable clothes
   - ☐ a plane ticket

B Give advice to these people. Use the words or phrases in the box and the items in part A. Use each word or phrase only once.

| ☐ ought to | ☐ need to | ☐ should | ✓ had better ('d better) |

1. Yuko is going on a vacation to a foreign country.
   She'd better take a passport.

2. Michelle and Steven are going on a mountain-climbing vacation.
   _____

3. Philip and Julia are planning a sailing trip.
   _____

4. Jack is going to visit a temple.
   _____

7 **You don't need to take that!**

Your friends are planning to drive
across North America and camp
along the way. What advice can you
give them? Write eight sentences
using the expressions in the box
and some of the cues below.

> You don't have to . . .   You ought to . . .
> You have to . . .   You should . . .
> You must . . .   You shouldn't . . .
> You need to . . .   You'd better . . .

bring cooking equipment   pack a lot of luggage
buy good quality camping equipment   remember to bring insect spray
buy maps and travel guides   remember to bring a jacket
forget a first-aid kit   take a credit card
forget your passport or identification take a lot of cash
get a GPS device for your car   take your driver's license

1. _You have to bring cooking equipment._

2. _____

3. _____

4. _____

5. _____

6. _____

7. _____

8. _____

8 **Rewrite these sentences. Find another way to say each sentence using the words given.**

1. I'm not going to go on vacation on my own. (alone)

   _____

2. I don't want to travel with anyone. (by myself)

   _____

3. You ought to travel with a friend. (should)

   _____

4. It's necessary to get a vaccination. (must)

   _____

9 *I'm going on vacation!*

A Read these notes, and then write a description of your vacation. Use *be going to* for the plans you've decided on. Use *will* with *maybe*, *probably*, *I guess*, or *I think* for the plans you're not sure about.

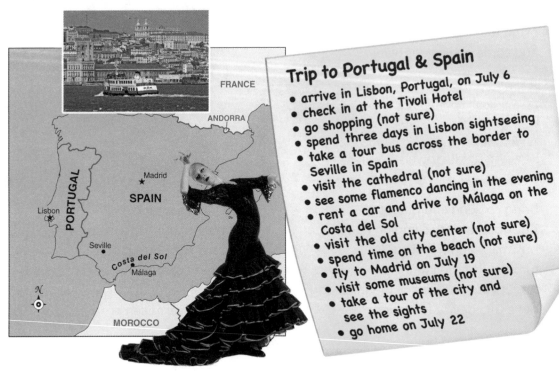

Trip to Portugal & Spain

- arrive in Lisbon, Portugal, on July 6
- check in at the Tivoli Hotel
- go shopping (not sure)
- spend three days in Lisbon sightseeing
- take a tour bus across the border to Seville in Spain
- visit the cathedral (not sure)
- see some flamenco dancing in the evening
- rent a car and drive to Málaga on the Costa del Sol
- visit the old city center (not sure)
- spend time on the beach (not sure)
- fly to Madrid on July 19
- visit some museums (not sure)
- take a tour of the city and see the sights
- go home on July 22

I'm going to arrive in Lisbon, Portugal, on July 6 and check in at the
Tivoli Hotel. Then maybe I'll go shopping. . . .

_____

_____

_____

_____

_____

_____

_____

_____

B Write five things you need to remember before you go on vacation.

1. I have to print my boarding pass.
2. _____
3. _____
4. _____
5. _____

OK. No problem!

1 *Write responses to these requests. Use* it *or* them.

1. Please take out the trash.

   <u>OK, I'll take it out.</u>

2. Please put the dishes away.

   _____

3. Hang up the towels.

   _____

4. Turn off the lights, please.

   _____

5. Turn on the radio.

   _____

2 *Two-part verbs*

A Use the words in the box to make two-part verbs. (You may use words more than once.)

away	down	off	on	out	up

1. clean ___up___
2. hang _____
3. let _____
4. pick _____
5. put _____

6. take _____
7. take _____
8. throw _____
9. turn _____
10. turn _____

B Make requests with the two-part verbs in part A. Then give a reason for making the request.

1. <u>Please clean up your room. It's dirty.</u>
2. _____
3. _____
4. _____
5. _____

3 Choose the correct word.

1. Hang up your _____coat_____ . (books / coat / trash)

2. Take out the _____ . (groceries / trash / yard)

3. Turn down the _____ . (garbage / TV / toys)

4. Pick up your _____ . (lights / things / yard)

5. Put away your _____ . (clothes / microwave / dog)

6. Turn on the _____ . (magazines / mess / radio)

4 What's your excuse?

A Complete these requests. Use the sentences in the box.

☐ It's a mess.   ☑ They shouldn't be on the floor.
☐ It's too loud.   ☐ The milk is getting warm.
☐ They're dirty.

1. Pick up your clothes, please. _They shouldn't be on the floor._

2. Please put the groceries away. _____

3. Take your shoes off. _____

4. Clean up the kitchen, please. _____

5. Turn down the music. _____

B Write an excuse for each request in part A.

1. _Sorry, but there isn't enough room in my closet._

2. _____

3. _____

4. _____

5. _____

5 Chores, chores, chores

A Scan the article. What are some ways to get children to do chores?

Helping out at home

In many families, household chores can be a problem. Who does them? Who should do them? In the past, many women stayed at home and did all the chores. Husbands went out to work and expected their wives to clean and cook. Nowadays, though, more and more women have jobs outside the home. So most people think that both wives and husbands should share responsibility for doing household chores. But what about kids? Should children help their parents around the house? If so, how old should they be when they start? How often should they help? And should they get money for helping?

Many people agree that children should help around the house. Doing chores is one way that children can learn to take responsibility for the mess they make. Some even say that young children should help in the home. They can do easy jobs – a child of six or seven years old, for example, can help do the laundry by separating dark-colored and light-colored clothes.

One problem is making sure that children and teenagers help regularly with chores. To solve this problem, some people suggest making a list of household chores, either on paper or on a computer spreadsheet. The list can have four parts: daily chores (such as doing the dishes), weekly chores (washing the car), monthly chores (cleaning the refrigerator), and yearly chores (cleaning the garage). Another suggestion to make sure that children do jobs around the house is to pay them. Some people say that this helps children and teenagers learn how to manage money, but others think it's wrong to pay kids to help because they are part of the family. After all, no one pays Mom or Dad to do the chores!

B Read the article. Then answer these questions.

1. Why do some people think that both wives and husbands should do household chores?

_____

2. Why do many people think that children should do some chores?

_____

3. What kinds of chores can young children do?

_____

4. What reasons are given for and against paying young people to do chores?

_____

_____

_____

6 Rewrite these sentences. Find another way to say each sentence using the words given.

1. Turn off your cell phone, please. (Can)

   <u>Can you turn off your cell phone, please?</u>

2. Take this form to the office. (Would you mind)

   _____

3. Please turn the TV down. (Could)

   _____

4. Don't leave wet towels on the floor. (Would you mind)

   _____

5. Text me today's homework assignment. (Would)

   _____

6. Pass me that book, please. (Can)

   _____

7 Choose the correct responses.

1. A: Could you lend me some money?

   B: <u>Sure.</u>
   - Sure.
   - Oh, sorry.
   - No, thanks.

2. A: Would you mind helping me?

   B: _____
   - Sorry, I can't right now.
   - No, thanks.
   - I forgot.

3. A: Excuse me, but you're sitting in my seat.

   B: _____
   - I'll close it.
   - Not right now.
   - Oh, I'm sorry. I didn't realize that.

4. A: Would you like to come in?

   B: _____
   - That's no excuse.
   - Sorry, I forgot.
   - All right. Thanks.

5. A: Would you mind not leaving your dirty

   clothes on the floor?

   B: _____
   - OK, thanks.
   - Oh, all right. I'll put them away.
   - Excuse me. I'll pay for them.

6. A: Can you hand me the remote control?

   B: _____
   - No problem.
   - You could, too.
   - I'll make sure.

8 For each complaint, apologize and either give an excuse, admit a mistake, make an offer, or make a promise.

1. Customer: This steak is very tough. I can't eat it.

   Waiter: _Oh, I'm sorry. I'll get you another one._

2. Steven: You're late! I've been here for half an hour!

   Katie: _____

3. Roommate 1: Could you turn the TV down?
   I'm trying to study, and the noise is bothering me.

   Roommate 2: _____

4. Father: You didn't take out the garbage this morning.

   Son: _____

5. Customer: I brought this laptop in last week,
   but it's still not working right.

   Salesperson: _____

6. Neighbor 1: Could you do something about your dog?
   It barks all night and keeps me awake.

   Neighbor 2: _____

7. Resident: Would you mind moving your car?
   You're parked in my parking space.

   Visitor: _____

8. Teacher: Please put away your papers. You left them on
   your desk yesterday.

   Student: _____

9 Choose the correct words.

1. Throw those empty bottles away.

   Put them in the _____ (recycling bin / living room / refrigerator).

2. Would you mind picking up some _____

   (dry cleaning / groceries / towels)? We need coffee, milk, and rice.

3. Turn the _____ (faucet / oven / stereo) off. Water

   costs money!

4. My neighbor made a _____ (mistake / request / promise).

   He said, "I'll be sure to stop my dog from barking."

10 ▪ Requests

A Match the words and phrases in columns A and B.

A	B	
☑ pick up	☐ your bedroom	1. <u>pick up some milk</u>
☐ not criticize	☑ some milk	2. _____
☐ mail	☐ the groceries	3. _____
☐ not talk	☐ your sunglasses	4. _____
☐ put away	☐ these bills	5. _____
☐ take off	☐ the TV	6. _____
☐ turn down	☐ so loudly	7. _____
☐ clean up	☐ my friends	8. _____

B Write requests using the phrases in part A.

1. <u>Would you mind picking up some milk?</u>

2. _____

3. _____

4. _____

5. _____

6. _____

7. _____

8. _____

11 *Write five complaints you have about a friend or a relative. Then write a wish for each complaint.*

1. My roommate is always using my hair dryer.

   <u>I wish she had her own hair dryer.</u>

2. _____

   _____

3. _____

   _____

4. _____

   _____

5. _____

   _____

7 What's this for?

1 *What are these items used for? Write a sentence about each item using* **used for** *and the information in the box.*

☐ do boring jobs   ☐ store and transmit data   ☐ transmit radio and TV programs

☑ write reports   ☐ determine your exact location

---

1 computer   **2** robot   **3** satellite   **4** flash drive   **5** GPS device

1. A computer is used for writing reports.

2. _____

3. _____

4. _____

5. _____

2 *Check (✓) the technology and what it does. Then write sentences using* **be used to.**

1. ☑ text messages   ☑ cell phone   ☐ photocopies

    A cell phone is used to send text messages.

2. ☐ MP4 player   ☐ videos   ☐ voice

    _____

3. ☐ games   ☐ satellites   ☐ weather

    _____

4. ☐ videos   ☐ messages   ☐ video camera

    _____

5. ☐ the Internet   ☐ robots   ☐ information

    _____

3 Choose the correct word to complete each sentence.
Use the correct form of the word.

1. Robots are used to _____perform_____ (find / perform / study) many dangerous jobs.

2. Computers are used to _____ (connect / download / sing) music.

3. Satellites are used for _____ (check / transmit / write) radio programs.

4. Home computers are used to _____ (play / pay / have) bills.

5. External hard drives are used for _____ (back up / email / buy) data.

6. Airport scanners are used to _____ (hide / allow / find) dangerous items.

4 Complete the sentences with **used to, is used to,** *or* **are used to.**

1. My sister _____used to_____ visit me on weekends when I was in college.

2. People _____ write letters, but nowadays they usually send emails instead.

3. A cell phone _____ make calls and send texts.

4. I _____ have a desktop computer, but now I just use a laptop.

5. We download all of our movies. We _____ buy DVDs, but not anymore.

6. Wi-Fi networks _____ access the Internet wirelessly.

5 *Garage sales*

A Scan these ads for garage sales. Which ones include electronics?

Garage Sales This Weekend

Next Week >

A **HOUSEHOLD** goods, including refrigerator, dishwasher, microwave oven, TV, stereo, couch, 2 bikes. Sat. 9–3. 1528 Williams Dr. Remember to bring cash only!

B **MOVING!** Office supplies, books, shelves, desk and office chair, and lots of old CDs! Sat. 8–3. 32 Harbor Rd.

C **VALUABLE** Mexican paintings, antique chairs, oriental rugs, collection of old Japanese kimonos and other clothes from around the world, old maps, gold coins. Sun. 11–5. 2039 E. 8th St. Try to arrive early!

D **COLLECTOR GOES BROKE!** Everything must go! Collection of shells, stamps, and coins from around the world, old postcards, photos. Sun. noon to 7. 9734 Date St. Make sure to tell your friends.

E **ELECTRICAL** engineer retiring. Laptop computers, cable modems, laser printers, fax machine, software for word processing and creating budgets, even a few video games. 9–5 Sat. & Sun. 2561 Canada Dr.

B Read the ads. Which garage sale should these people attend? (More than one answer may be possible.)

1. _____ Linda has just started her own business. She likes to play music while she works.

2. _____ Edmund and Tina decorate homes. They always use old and unusual items to make the houses they decorate more interesting.

3. _____ James needs some furniture for his new apartment.

4. _____ Rebecca wants to have an office in her home.

5. _____ Sam likes collecting interesting and unusual things from different countries.

6 *Useful types of websites*

A Match the types of websites with how people use them.

Types of websites	How people use websites
_e_ answer sites	a. find out what's happening in the world
_____ blogs	b. share information and photos with friends
_____ dating sites	c. find information on the Internet
_____ gaming sites	d. write and edit web pages
_____ media sharing sites	e. ask and answer questions online
_____ news sites	f. find a partner
_____ search engines	g. play online games
_____ social networking sites	h. post online diaries
_____ wiki sites	i. upload videos and music

B Do you use any of the types of websites in part A? What do you use them for? Write sentences.

1. I use answer sites to ask and answer questions online. _____ OR

   I use answer sites for asking and answering questions online. _____

2. _____

3. _____

4. _____

 7 *Put these instructions in order. Number them from 1 to 5.*

← →   **Social Networking**   Search

Getting Started with Social Networking

_____ Next, check what the site has to offer you. Don't worry if you can't understand all its functions.

_____ First of all, join a social networking site. Choose a site where you already know people.

_____ After that, use the site's search features to find friends. Be sure to browse through groups who share your interests.

_____ Finally, invite people to be your friend. Try not to be shy! Lots of people may be waiting to hear from you.

_____ Then customize your profile page. For example, play with the colors to make the page reflect your personality. Now you're ready to start exploring!

8 Write a sentence about each picture using an expression in the box.

☐ Be sure to . . .   ☑ Make sure to . . .   ☐ Try not to . . .
☐ Don't forget to . . .   ☐ Remember to . . .   ☐ Try to . . .

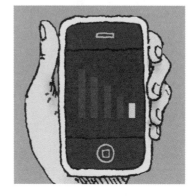

1. Make sure to turn off your computer.

2. _____

3. _____

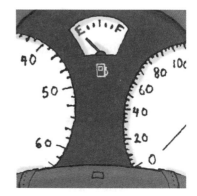

4. _____

5. _____

6. _____

9 Write *a* or *an* in the correct places. (There are nine other places in this paragraph.)

My brother just bought ^*a* smartphone. It's really great. It has lot of high-tech features. In fact, it's amazing handheld computer, not just cell phone. For example, it has Wi-Fi connectivity, so my brother can connect to the Internet in most places. He can send message to friend by email or through social networking site. He can also find out where he is because it has GPS app. That's perfect for my brother because he likes mountain climbing. He'll never get lost again! His smartphone also has excellent camera, so he can take photos of his climbing trips. And, of course, it's phone. So he can talk to his girlfriend anytime he wants!

10 *Rewrite these sentences. Find another way to say each sentence using the words given.*

1. I use my computer for paying bills. (online)

   I pay my bills online.

2. It breaks very easily. (fragile)

   _____

3. Take it out of the outlet. (unplug)

   _____

4. Remember to keep it dry. (spill)

   _____

5. Don't let the battery die. (recharge)

   _____

 11 *Look at the pictures and complete this conversation. Choose the correct responses.*

A: What a day! First, my microwave didn't work.

B: What happened?

A: It burned my lunch.

    • It didn't cook my lunch.
    • It burned my lunch.

    Then I tried to use my computer,

    but that didn't work either.

B: Why not?

A: _____

    • I couldn't get a Wi-Fi signal.
    • I couldn't turn it on.

    After that, I tried to use the vacuum cleaner.

B: Let me guess. It didn't pick up the dirt.

A: Worse! _____

    • It made a terrible noise.
    • It spread dirt around the room.

B: Did you have your robot help?

A: Well, I tried to get it to clean the outside

    windows. _____

    • But it refused.
    • It did a great job.

B: I don't blame it! You live on the 50th floor!

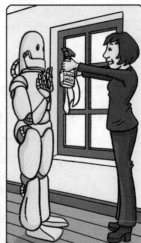

8 Let's celebrate!

1 **Complete this paragraph with the words in the box.**

- ☐ celebrate
- ☐ customs
- ☐ fireworks
- ☐ get-togethers
- ✓ holidays
- ☐ music
- ☐ picnic
- ☐ streamers

One of the most important national ___holidays___ in the United States is Independence Day. This is the day when Americans _____ winning their independence from Britain almost 250 years ago. There are many _____ for Independence Day. Most towns, big and small, mark this holiday with parades and _____ . They decorate with lots of _____ , usually in red, white, and blue, the colors of the U.S. flag. Bands play patriotic _____ . It's also a day when many Americans have family _____ . Families celebrate with a barbecue or a _____ .

2 **Complete the sentences with the clauses in the box.**

- ☐ when I feel sad and depressed
- ☐ when people have to pay their taxes
- ☐ when school starts
- ☐ when summer vacation begins

1. I hate April 15! In the United States, it's the day _____ . I always owe the government money.

2. June is my favorite month. It's the month _____ _____ . I always head straight for the beach.

3. September is my least favorite month. It's the month _____ . Good-bye, summer!

4. I have never liked winter. It's a season _____ . The cold weather always affects my mood negatively.

3 *Crossword puzzle: Special days*

Use words from the unit to complete the crossword puzzle.

Across

4 _____ is the time of year when there are a lot of weddings in the U.S.

5 People like to play _____ on each other on April Fools' Day.

6 We always have a _____ at our house on New Year's Eve.

8 On Labor Day, people in the U.S. _____ workers.

9 Janice and Nick are getting married soon. They plan to have a small _____ with just a few family members.

11 My friends and family gave me some very nice _____ on my birthday.

14 People waited along the route for hours to see the _____ pass through the streets.

15 I gave my grandmother a bouquet of _____ on Mother's Day.

16 People in the United States and Canada celebrate the _____ at Thanksgiving.

Down

1 Everyone in my family eats _____ on Thanksgiving.

2 Hurry up with the balloons and the streamers! We need to finish the _____ before our guests arrive.

3 To celebrate the new year, many people shoot _____ into the air at night.

7 Tomorrow is my parents' twenty-fifth wedding _____ .

10 November 2 is the day when my family and I go to the cemetery to clean the _____ of our ancestors.

12 My favorite _____ are spring and summer.

13 I send my friends _____ on special occasions.

4 *A lot to celebrate!*

A Read about these special days in the United States.
Do you celebrate any of them in your country?

EVENT	DAY	HOW PEOPLE CELEBRATE IT
Martin Luther King Jr. Day	3rd Monday in January	This is the day people honor the life and work of the civil rights leader Martin Luther King Jr.
Presidents' Day	3rd Monday in February	This day honors two great presidents of the United States, George Washington and Abraham Lincoln.
April Fools' Day	April 1	This is a day when people play tricks on friends. Websites sometimes post funny stories or advertise fake products.
Earth Day	April 22	This is a day when people think about protecting the earth. People give speeches about ways to help take care of the environment.
Mother's Day	2nd Sunday in May	People honor their mothers by giving cards and gifts and having a family gathering.
Father's Day	2nd Sunday in June	People honor their fathers by giving them cards and presents.
Independence Day	July 4	Americans celebrate their country's independence from Britain. There are parades and fireworks.
Labor Day	1st Monday in September	People honor workers and celebrate the end of summer. Most people have the day off, and they have barbecues with friends and family.

B Complete the chart. Check (✓) the correct answers.

	Americans give each other gifts on:	Americans don't give gifts on:
Martin Luther King Jr. Day	☐	☐
Presidents' Day	☐	☐
April Fools' Day	☐	☐
Earth Day	☐	☐
Mother's Day	☐	☐
Father's Day	☐	☐
Independence Day	☐	☐
Labor Day	☐	☐

5 **What happens at these times in your country? Complete the sentences.**

1. Before a man and woman get married, they
   usually date each other.

2. When someone has a birthday, _____

   _____

3. Before some people eat a meal, _____

   _____

4. After a student graduates, _____

   _____

5. When a woman gets engaged, _____

   _____

6. When a couple has their first child, _____

   _____

7. When a person retires, _____

   _____

6 **Complete the paragraph with the information in the box.**
Add a comma where necessary.

> **Grammar note: Adverbial clauses of time**
>
> **The adverbial clause can come before or after the main clause.**
> **Before the main clause, add a comma.**
> When a couple gets married, they often receive gifts.
> **Do not add a comma after the main clause.**
> A couple often receives gifts when they get married.

- [ ] before the wedding reception ends
- [ ] many newlyweds have to live with relatives
- [ ] most couples like to be alone
- [ ] when they have enough money to pay for it

Newly married couples often leave on their honeymoon _____

_____ . When they go on their

honeymoon _____ .

After they come back from their honeymoon _____

_____ . They can only live in their own place

_____ .

7 Write three paragraphs about marriage customs in your country.
In the first paragraph, write about what happens before the wedding.
In the second paragraph, write about the wedding ceremony.
In the final paragraph, write about what happens after the wedding.

_____

_____

_____

_____

_____

_____

_____

_____

_____

_____

Japan

Morocco

Scotland

India

8 Choose the correct word or phrase.

1. Wedding _____ (celebrations / flowers / birthdays) are often held in a restaurant or hotel.

2. Children's Day is a day when people in many countries _____ (court / honor / occur) their children.

3. Fall is the _____ (custom / get-together / season) when North Americans celebrate Thanksgiving.

4. In Indonesia, on Nyepi Day, Balinese people _____ (last / eat / observe) a day of silence to begin the new year.

9 *Rewrite these sentences. Find another way to say each sentence using the words given.*

1. Everyone in the family comes to my parents' home on Thanksgiving. (get together)

   Everyone in the family gets together at my parents' home on Thanksgiving.

2. Many people have parties on New Year's Eve. (New Year's Eve / when)

   _____

3. At the end of the year, Japanese people give and receive *oseibo* presents to show their appreciation for the people in their lives. (exchange)

   _____

4. June is the month when many Brazilians celebrate the Festa Junina. (in June)

   _____

5. In Sweden, people observe Midsummer's Day around June 21. (occur)

   _____

10 *Imagine you are in a foreign country and someone has invited you to a New Year's Eve party. Ask questions about the party using the words in the box or your own ideas.*

☐ clothes	☐ midnight	☐ sing and dance
☐ fireworks	☑ present	☐ special food or drink

1. *Should I bring a New Year's present?* _____

2. _____

3. _____

4. _____

5. _____

6. _____